How to Be A Facility Manager
A Beginner's Guide to the Essentials of Facility Management
Nicholas Czak

Copyright © 2024 Nicholas Czak

All rights reserved.

No portion of this book may be reproduced in any form without written permission from the publisher or author, except as permitted by U.S. copyright law.

Contents

1. Unveiling the World of Facility Management   1
2. Demystifying Facility Management   15
3. Groundwork Essentials   24
4. Beyond On-the-Job Learning   31
5. From Jack-of-All-Trades to Master: 43
6. Financial Acumen   55
7. Contracts and Vendors   68
8. Navigating Career Progression   80
9. Leadership Essentials   94
10. Operations and Maintenance   102
11. Tenant and Occupant Relations: 112
12. Environmental Stewardship: 124
13. Technology and Automation   131
14. Compliance and Risk Mitigation   144
15. Continuous Learning   160

16.	Mentorship	170
17.	Embarking on Your Facility Management Odyssey	178

Chapter 1
Unveiling the World of Facility Management
A High-Level Orientation

Welcome to the dynamic and strategic world of facility management (FM)! Whether you're a seasoned pro or a curious newcomer, understanding the core concepts lays a solid foundation for your journey. Buckle up, as we unveil the key areas that you'll navigate as a facility manager, equipped with industry terms, FAQs, pros and cons, and actionable takeaways.

The Essential Pillars:

Imagine yourself as the maestro of a complex symphony. Each instrument represents a crucial pillar of FM:

1. **Space:** You're the guardian of physical environments, from sprawling campuses to compact co-working spaces. Understanding their **floor plans, HVAC systems, ADA compliance**, and **space optimization** is essential.

2. **People:** From employees and residents to visitors and vendors, people are the heart of your facility. Ensuring their **comfort, safety, and well-being** through **emergency preparedness, access control, and occupant well-being initiatives** is paramount.

3. **Processes:** Efficient workflows keep your facility humming. Think **preventive maintenance, energy management, waste reduction, and data-driven decision-making**. Mastering these processes translates to **optimizing costs, minimizing downtime, and maximizing efficiency**.

Wearing Multiple Hats:

Get ready to be a multi-talented leader! As a facility manager, you'll:

- **Become a maintenance wiz:** Master **preventive maintenance schedules, oversee repairs, and manage emergency response plans.** Think **HVAC upkeep, plumbing repairs, and fire safety protocols.**

- **Transform into an operational maestro:** Juggle tasks like **budgeting, cost control, procurement, and regulatory compliance.** Optimize **energy consumption, waste management, and sustainability initiatives.**

- **Embrace the tech wizard:** Leverage **building automation systems, data analytics, and IoT solutions** to streamline operations and monitor performance. Become familiar with terms like **BMS, BIM, and IIoT.**

- **Sharpen your communication skills:** Collaborate effectively with diverse stakeholders - occupants, contractors, and leadership - through clear and concise communication. **Negotiation, conflict resolution, and stakeholder engagement** are key.

- **Become a project management pro:** From

minor renovations to major upgrades, oversee projects with **budgeting, scheduling, and risk management**, ensuring timely completion and minimal disruption. Familiarize yourself with **critical path method (CPM) and Agile methodologies**.

Beyond the Basics:

While the core pillars remain constant, FM adapts to specific contexts. Consider specializing in areas like:

- **Healthcare facilities:** Navigate specialized regulations and equipment needs for patient care.

- **Educational institutions:** Ensure safety and foster learning environments for students and staff.

- **Commercial properties:** Cater to tenant needs and maximize return on investment for owners.

The Evolving Landscape:

Staying ahead of the curve is crucial in this dynamic field. Here's what's shaping the future:

- **Sustainability:** Minimize environmental impact through **green building practices, renewable energy, and waste reduction**.

- **Technology:** Embrace innovations like **AI-powered predictive maintenance, smart buildings, and digital twins**.

- **Changing demographics:** Adapt facilities to accommodate diverse needs and evolving workstyles, like **flexible workspaces and accessibility considerations**.

- **Regulations:** Stay updated on evolving **building codes, safety standards, and environmental regulations**.

FAQs for Aspiring Facility Managers:

- **What's a typical day like?** Every day is different! Expect problem-solving, project management, communication, and strategic planning.

- **What skills are essential?** Strong communication, leadership, analytical thinking, problem-solving, and technical aptitude are key.

- **What education and certifications are needed?** A bachelor's degree in FM, business, or engineering is common. Certifications like CFM (Certified Facility Manager) enhance your profile.

- **What are the career prospects?** The field is growing rapidly, offering ample opportunities for advancement and diverse specializations.

Pros and Cons of Being a Facility Manager:

Pros:

- **Variety and challenge:** Every day brings new problems to solve and keeps you on your toes.

- **Making a difference:** Your work directly impacts the comfort, safety, and productivity of occupants.

- **Dynamic and evolving field:** Continuous learning and adapting to new technologies keeps your career exciting.

- **Good job security:** The demand for skilled facility managers is high and growing.

Cons:

- **Stressful and demanding:** Deadlines, emergencies, and unexpected challenges are part of the job.

- **Long hours:** Be prepared to work evenings and weekends when necessary.

- **Constant learning:** Keeping up with evolving technologies and regulations requires ongoing effort.

- **Can be physically demanding:** Depending on your facility, some tasks involve physical exertion.

Action Items:

- **Shadow a facility manager:** Get firsthand experience by shadowing a professional in your desired specialization.

- **Consider certifications:** Explore options like CFM, LEED AP, or specialized certifications relevant to your interests.

- **Network with industry professionals:** Attend industry events, join online communities, and connect with peers to learn and build relationships.

- **Start building your skills:** Take online courses, read industry publications, and volunteer for projects that utilize relevant skills.

- **Research salary and job market trends:** Get informed about potential earning potential and career paths in different sectors.

- **Identify your strengths and interests:** Reflect on what motivates you and where you can add value within the FM field.

- **Develop your personal brand:** Craft a strong online presence and showcase your relevant skills and experiences.

- **Start building your portfolio:** Document projects, achievements, and skills relevant to FM career goals.

- **Don't be afraid to start small:** Look for entry-level positions or internships to gain practical experience and build your resume.

- **Remember, continuous learning is key:** Stay updated on industry trends, technologies, and best practices throughout your career.

By taking these action steps, you can embark on your journey towards a rewarding and fulfilling career in facility management. Remember, the world of FM is vast and offers diverse opportunities. Find your niche, embrace the challenges, and make a positive impact on the spaces you manage!

Bonus Tip:

Develop your "soft skills." Effective communication, interpersonal skills, critical thinking, and problem-solving abilities are essential for success in any career, but especially in FM. These skills will enable you to collaborate effectively with diverse stakeholders, manage conflict constructively, and navigate the complex challenges of managing a facility.

Bonus Bonus Section: FM Across Diverse Landscapes

The diverse nature of facilities demands versatility from their managers. While the core principles remain constant, the specific skills and responsibilities will adapt to your environment. Let's explore how:

Commercial/Industrial Plants & Factories:

- **Master process optimization:** Ensure production efficiency by maintaining critical machinery, managing utilities, and implementing lean manufacturing principles.

- **Embrace industrial safety:** Become well-versed in OSHA regulations, hazard identification, and emergency response protocols.

- **Understand industrial automation:** Familiarize yourself with terms like SCADA, DCS, and IIoT for effective maintenance and integration.

- **Common synonymous titles:** Plant Engineer, Maintenance Manager, Operations Manager.

Small Properties & Boutique Hotels:

- **Be a jack-of-all-trades:** Master diverse tasks like plumbing, electrical repairs, HVAC upkeep, and basic carpentry.

- **Cultivate exceptional interpersonal skills:** Provide personalized service to tenants or guests, fostering a positive and welcoming environment.

- **Embrace budget consciousness:** Optimize resource allocation and explore cost-saving measures in a smaller setting.

- **Common synonymous titles:** Building Manager, Property Manager, Hotel Operations Manager.

Healthcare Facilities:

- **Navigate stringent regulations:** Ensure compliance with HIPAA, Joint Commission standards, and other healthcare-specific codes.

- **Prioritize infection control:** Implement rigorous sanitation protocols and maintain sterile environments.

- **Understand medical equipment:** Familiarize yourself with specialized equipment and maintenance procedures.

- **Common synonymous titles:** Facilities Director, Biomedical Equipment Technician, Environmental Services Manager.

Educational Institutions:

- **Foster a safe learning environment:** Maintain playgrounds, ensure fire safety compliance, and implement emergency preparedness plans.

- **Optimize learning spaces:** Adapt classrooms and common areas to meet evolving pedagogical needs and accessibility standards.

- **Manage diverse facilities:** From libraries and laboratories to athletic fields, each requires specialized knowledge and maintenance strategies.

- **Common synonymous titles:** School Facilities Manager, Campus Operations Director, Maintenance Supervisor.

Remember, these are just a few examples. The possibilities are endless!

Additional Industry Terms:

- **LEED:** Leadership in Energy and Environmental Design (green building certification)

- **BIM:** Building Information Modeling (3D digital representation of a building)

- **CMMS:** Computerized Maintenance Management System

- **HVAC:** Heating, Ventilation, and Air Conditioning

- **ADA:** Americans with Disabilities Act (accessibility standards)

- **NFPA:** National Fire Protection Association (fire safety standards)

Final Thought:

Facility management is a dynamic and rewarding career path offering diverse challenges and opportunities. Identify your interests, leverage your skills, and embrace the ever-evolving landscape. This handbook has provided a roadmap, but your journey continues as you explore, adapt, and shape the future of your chosen facility!

Chapter 2
Demystifying Facility Management
: Understanding the Landscape and Your Role

Welcome to the world of facility management! Whether you're a seasoned professional or just starting out, navigating this vast and multifaceted field can feel overwhelming. This chapter aims to demystify facility management, providing a comprehensive overview of the landscape and your potential role within it.

1.1 What is Facility Management?

Imagine the buildings, offices, factories, hospitals, and campuses that hum with daily activity. Facility management is the invisible force behind their smooth operation. It encompasses a wide range of activities, from **maintaining the physical infrastructure** (think HVAC systems, plumbing, electrical) to **creating a safe and comfortable work environment** (lighting, acoustics, space planning) to **supporting the core business needs of the organization**.

1.2 The Diverse Landscape:

Facility management is present in nearly every industry, adapting to unique needs across different sectors. Here's a glimpse into the variety:

- **Corporate:** High-rise offices, data centers, and research facilities demand cutting-edge technology and efficient space utilization.

- **Healthcare:** Hospitals, clinics, and laboratories require specific hygiene standards, safety protocols, and specialized equipment maintenance.

- **Education:** Schools, universities, and libraries need to cater to diverse needs, from classrooms and labs to sports facilities and student housing.

- **Retail:** Shopping malls, grocery stores, and restaurants require specific aesthetics, customer comfort, and inventory management considerations.

- **Manufacturing:** Factories and production facilities demand precision in maintaining machinery, ensuring safety, and optimizing workflow.

1.3 Understanding Your Role:

While the basic definitions provided offer a starting point, let's dive deeper into the diverse roles within facility management:

Facility Manager: Imagine the conductor of an orchestra, leading and coordinating the various aspects of the facility. Responsibilities include:

- **Strategic planning:** Setting long-term goals, aligning with organizational objectives, and developing budgets.

- **Staff management:** Leading and motivating teams, including operations, maintenance, and administrative personnel.

- **Contract management:** Overseeing relationships with vendors and service providers.

- **Compliance:** Ensuring adherence to all safety, environmental, and building regulations.

- **Data analysis:** Utilizing data to optimize operations, identify trends, and make informed decisions.

- **Technology integration:** Implementing and managing facility management software and technology solutions.

Operations Manager: Think of the stage manager, ensuring everything runs smoothly behind the scenes. Their focus includes:

- **Daily operations:** Overseeing cleaning, security, waste management, and other essential services.

- **Space management:** Optimizing space utilization, handling tenant requests, and managing furniture and equipment.

- **Work order management:** Scheduling and supervising maintenance tasks, ensuring timely completion.

- **Communication:** Coordinating with internal and external stakeholders, addressing concerns, and providing updates.

- **Emergency preparedness:** Developing and implementing emergency response plans and procedures.

Maintenance Technician: They are the skilled hands-on crew, keeping the facility running smoothly. Their tasks include:

- **Preventative maintenance:** Performing routine inspections, servicing equipment, and identifying potential issues.

- **Corrective maintenance:** Repairing equipment breakdowns, troubleshooting problems, and restoring functionality.

- **Work order completion:** Executing work orders efficiently and documenting repairs accurately.

- **Safety compliance:** Following safety protocols, using personal protective equipment (PPE), and reporting hazards.

- **Staying up-to-date:** Continuously learning and acquiring new skills as technology and equipment evolve.

Project Manager: The architect of change, overseeing capital improvement projects within the facility. Their duties encompass:

- **Project planning:** Defining project scope, timelines, budgets, and resource allocation.

- **Communication:** Collaborating with stakeholders, managing expectations, and communicating progress.

- **Risk management:** Identifying and mitigating potential risks, ensuring project success.

- **Quality control:** Monitoring project execution, ensuring adherence to specifications and quality standards.

- **Budget management:** Controlling project costs, staying within budget, and identifying opportunities for savings.

Sustainability Coordinator: The eco-champion, responsible for minimizing the facility's environmental impact. Their tasks include:

- **Developing and implementing sustainability initiatives:** Energy efficiency projects, waste reduction programs, and water conservation measures.

- **Data analysis and reporting:** Monitoring energy consumption, waste generation, and other environmental metrics.

- **Promoting sustainability awareness:** Educating employees and tenants about sustainable practices.

- **Compliance with environmental regulations:** Ensuring adherence to relevant environmental laws and policies.

- **Partnerships and collaboration:** Building relationships with sustainability organizations and vendors.

Remember, these are just general descriptions, and specific roles can vary depending on the size, industry, and complexity of the facility.

Remember: Each role plays a crucial part in the symphony of facility management, working together to create a safe, efficient, and sustainable environment for occupants and the organization.

1.4 Essential Skills for Success:

Regardless of your specific role, certain skills are crucial for success in facility management:

- **Strong communication and interpersonal skills:** Collaboration with stakeholders, tenants, and service providers is key.

- **Problem-solving and analytical skills:** Troubleshooting issues, making decisions, and finding efficient solutions are essential.

- **Project management skills:** Planning, organizing, and executing projects within budget and timeline is crucial.

- **Financial literacy:** Understanding budgets, cost control, and resource allocation is important.

- **Technical knowledge:** Basic understanding of building systems, maintenance procedures, and technology is beneficial.

1.5 The Future of Facility Management:

Facility management is evolving rapidly, driven by technology advancements, sustainability concerns, and changing workplace dynamics. Trends to watch include:

- **Integration of IoT and smart building technologies for automation and data-driven de-**

cision making.

- **Increased focus on occupant well-being and experience, optimizing workspaces for health and productivity.**

- **Sustainability initiatives, reducing energy consumption and environmental impact.**

- **Greater use of data analytics to predict maintenance needs and optimize operations.**

Conclusion:

This chapter has provided a foundational understanding of facility management, its diverse landscape, and your potential role within it. As you delve deeper, remember that continuous learning and adaptability are key to navigating this dynamic field and contributing to the efficient and sustainable operation of the built environment.

This is just the beginning! The following chapters will delve deeper into specific aspects of facility management, equipping you with the knowledge and skills to excel in your chosen path.

Chapter 3
Groundwork Essentials
From Technician to Tactician

You've mastered the intricacies of changing air filters, unclogging drains, and keeping the lights on. But facility management is more than just wrenches and mops. It's about understanding the bigger picture, strategizing effectively, and becoming a tactician, not just a technician. This chapter equips you with the essentials to build a solid foundation and transition from hands-on experience to strategic thinking.

Laying the Bricks: Technical Proficiency Matters

Your initial role honed valuable skills – fixing equipment, maintaining systems, and understanding building operations intimately. Remember, this technical expertise remains your bedrock. It allows you to:

- **Troubleshoot problems efficiently:** Your experience translates to faster diagnoses and solutions, minimizing downtime and ensuring smooth operations.

- **Communicate effectively with technicians and vendors:** You understand their language and challenges, fostering better collaboration and ensuring repairs are done right.

- **Gain credibility:** Your hands-on expertise commands respect and demonstrates a deep understanding of the facilities you manage.

Expanding Your Horizons: Beyond the Wrench

While technical prowess is crucial, growth requires venturing beyond daily tasks. Embrace the following:

- **Broaden your knowledge:** Explore different departments like HVAC, electrical, and groundskeeping. Learn their interconnectivity and gain insights into budgeting, scheduling, and communication within the facility team.

- **Shadow leaders and mentors:** Observe how experienced managers approach challenges, strategize solutions, and interact with stakeholders. Ask questions, soak up their knowledge, and learn from their successes and mistakes.

- **Seek formal training:** Enroll in online courses, industry certifications, or manufacturer training programs to acquire targeted knowledge in areas like project management, building automation, or sustainability.

Sharpening Your Tactical Skills:

As you expand your understanding, develop critical thinking and strategic abilities:

- **Analyze and prioritize:** Move beyond reactive fixes. Analyze recurring issues, prioritize preventive maintenance, and implement plans to avoid disruptions.

- **Cost-consciousness:** Understand budgetary constraints and identify opportunities for cost savings through efficient resource allocation and strategic procurement.

- **Data-driven decision-making:** Learn to interpret data collected from building systems and leverage it for informed decisions on maintenance, resource allocation, and energy efficiency.

Don't Just Learn on the Job, Train for It:

While valuable, "learning on the job" alone has limitations. Take charge of your development:

- **Network actively:** Attend industry events, join professional associations, and connect with experienced facility managers. Share experiences, learn from diverse perspectives, and seek mentorship.

- **Be proactive:** Don't wait for opportunities to come your way. Volunteer for challenging projects, suggest process improvements, and showcase your initiative and willingness to learn.

- **Document your achievements:** Track completed courses, certifications, and contributions to projects. This demonstrates your commitment to continuous learning and professional development.

Remember, the journey from technician to tactician is continuous. Embrace curiosity, actively seek growth opportunities, and leverage your technical knowledge to become a strategic thinker and valuable asset to the facility management team. You're not just fixing things; you're shaping the environment where people thrive and organizations succeed.

3 Real-World Examples of Technician to Manager Transitions:

1. From Electrician to Sustainability Champion:
- An electrical technician at a manufacturing facility identified recurring energy inefficiencies and suggested cost-saving solutions. Their initiative led to training in energy auditing and sustainable practices, eventually securing a position as Sustainability Manager after implementing successful energy-saving measures.

- **Key Takeaway:** Recognizing opportunities beyond daily tasks and demonstrating proactiveness can open doors to specialized roles.

2. From HVAC Technician to Technology Integrator:
- An HVAC technician saw the growing role of technology and enrolled in online courses on building automation systems. Utilizing their

newfound knowledge, they integrated smart controls and automated several systems, reducing energy consumption and improving efficiency, ultimately landing a position as a Technology Integration Specialist.

- **Key Takeaway:** Embracing emerging technologies and upskilling in relevant areas can create new career paths.

3. From Janitor to Operations Manager:
- A janitor in a large hospital went above and beyond, reporting potential maintenance issues, learning basic equipment operation, and demonstrating exceptional attention to detail. The facility manager recognized their potential and provided cross-training opportunities. Their dedication and willingness to learn led to a promotion as Operations Manager, overseeing daily operations and ensuring smooth facility functioning.

- **Key Takeaway:** A strong work ethic, dedication to learning, and taking initiative can lead to unexpected career advancements.

These examples showcase individuals from various technical backgrounds successfully transitioning to leadership roles in facility management. Their journeys highlight the importance of strategic thinking, continuous learning, and soft skills for career growth in this dynamic field.

Chapter 4
Beyond On-the-Job Learning
Sharpening Your Skills for the Big Leagues

You've mastered the daily grind, your wrench feels like an extension of your arm, and you know the building like the back of your hand. But to truly excel in facility management, you need to sharpen your skills for the big leagues. This chapter equips you with the knowledge and resources to move beyond on-the-job learning and strategically build your skillset for a successful career journey.

Limitations of "Learning by Doing"

While hands-on experience is invaluable, relying solely on "learning by doing" can limit your potential. Imagine entering a boxing ring without training – you might have the heart, but you'll lack the strategy and finesse to truly succeed. In facility management, similar limitations exist:

- **Limited Scope:** Daily tasks expose you only to a fragment of the bigger picture. You miss strategic planning, leadership nuances, and industry best practices.

- **Unstructured Learning:** Knowledge absorption is haphazard, relying on chance opportunities and who you shadow. Crucial areas like budgeting, communication, and project management might be neglected.

- **Reinforcing Biases:** You inherit existing practices, potentially outdated or inefficient, without critical evaluation or exposure to better approaches.

- **Slow Progression:** Advancement depends on attrition or someone recognizing your talent, a chance-driven and potentially lengthy process.

Sharpening Your Arsenal: Formal and Informal Learning

Break free from these limitations by actively seeking knowledge and refining your skillset. Embrace both formal and informal learning opportunities:

- **Formal Training:**

    - **Online courses:** Explore platforms like Coursera, EdX, and Udemy for targeted courses on facility management, finance, project management, or sustainability.

    - **Industry certifications:** Pursue certifications like CFM (Certified Facility Manager) or LEED AP O+M (Leadership in Energy and Environmental Design Accredited Professional: Operations + Maintenance) to demonstrate expertise and commitment.

    - **Manufacturer training:** Gain in-depth knowledge of specific equipment or systems through manufacturer-sponsored training programs.

- **Informal Learning:**

    - **Network actively:** Attend industry events,

join professional associations or BOMA (Building Owners and Managers Association), and connect with experienced facility managers. Share experiences, learn from diverse perspectives, and seek mentorship.

- **Shadowing Strategically:** Seek opportunities to shadow leaders across different departments, not just your immediate supervisor. Observe their approaches to challenges, communication styles, and decision-making processes.

- **Industry publications and podcasts:** Stay updated on trends, best practices, and emerging technologies through publications like Facility Management Journal or podcasts like The FM Buzz.

Building Your Champion Skillset:

Beyond technical expertise, hone essential skills for leading and managing effectively:

- **Communication:** Master clear, concise, and impactful communication, both written and verbal. Effective communication fosters collaboration, builds trust, and ensures smooth operations.

- **Teamwork:** Develop strong leadership skills to motivate, delegate, and build a positive team environment. Remember, your team is your greatest asset.

- **Problem-solving:** Approach challenges with critical thinking, creativity, and analytical skills. Find effective solutions that consider long-term impact and stakeholder needs.

- **Financial Acumen:** Understand budgeting principles, cost-saving strategies, and the financial implications of your decisions. Facility management is about efficiency and responsible resource allocation.

- **Technology Proficiency:** Embrace technology! Learn about building automation systems, data analytics, and other emerging tools to optimize operations and gain valuable insights.

Proactive Strategies for Success:

Don't wait for opportunities to come your way. Take charge of your development:

- **Document your achievements:** Track completed courses, certifications, and project contributions. This showcases your initiative and commitment to continuous learning.

- **Volunteer for challenging projects:** Step outside your comfort zone and demonstrate your willingness to learn and take on new responsibilities.

- **Be a self-advocate:** Articulate your career goals and actively seek opportunities for growth and advancement within your organization.

Remember, the journey from technician to tactician is a continuous process. Embrace lifelong learning, actively seek out new challenges, and leverage your diverse skillset to become a valuable asset in the exciting world of facility management. You're not just keeping the lights on; you're shaping the environment where people thrive and businesses succeed.

Here's your arsenal of formal and informal learning opportunities:

Formal Training:

- **Online courses:**

    - **Coursera Building Operations and Maintenance**

Certificate: https://www.coursera.org/lecture/supply-chain-principles/maintenance-operation-1RrAy - Deep-dive into maintenance planning, scheduling, and cost management.

- **EdX Introduction to Building Automation Systems:** https://www.edx.org/learn/automation - Master the technology transforming building operations.

- **Industry certifications:**

  - **Energy Star Certified Building Operations Professional**

  - **LEED AP Facility Operations + Maintenance**

- **Manufacturer training:** Gain in-depth knowledge of specific equipment or systems through programs like Johnson Controls' Building Automation University or Siemens Building Technologies Academy.

Informal Learning:

- **Network actively:**

  - Join and attend their events to connect with experienced professionals and learn from their journeys.

  - Participate in online forums like Facility Management Professionals Network or FM Link to connect with a wider community and engage in discussions.

  - Consider attending industry conferences like Facility Management Expo or BOMA International Convention for an immersive learning experience.

- **Shadowing strategically:**

  - Request to shadow leaders across departments like finance, project management, and sustainability to broaden your perspective.

  - Observe their decision-making processes, communication styles, and leadership approaches.

  - Ask insightful questions and actively seek

their mentorship.

- **Industry publications and podcasts:**

  - Stay informed by subscribing to Facility Management Journal, Buildings Magazine, or FM Talk podcast to learn about industry trends and best practices.

  - Follow thought leaders and influencers on social media for additional insights and inspiration.

Inspiring Stories of Transition:

- **From HVAC Technician to Sustainability Champion:** Sarah noticed recurring energy inefficiencies in her hospital and proposed cost-saving solutions. Her initiative led to training in energy auditing, and she eventually became the Sustainability Manager, implementing successful green initiatives.

- **From Electrician to Technology Integrator:** David saw the growing role of technology and enrolled in building automation courses. He integrated smart controls and automated systems, reducing energy consumption and earning a Technology Integration Specialist position.

- **From Janitor to Operations Manager:** Aisha's dedication and attention to detail were recognized by the facility manager. She received cross-training opportunities, showcasing her leadership potential and ultimately securing a promotion to Operations Manager.

Action Items for Your Success:
- **Identify your learning goals:** What specific skills do you want to develop? Are you aiming for a leadership role or specialization?

- **Create a personalized learning plan:** Choose relevant courses, certifications, and networking opportunities that align with your goals.

- **Set achievable milestones:** Break down your learning journey into smaller steps and track your progress to stay motivated.

- **Seek out mentors:** Find experienced facility managers who can guide and support your development.

- **Be proactive:** Don't wait for opportunities; volunteer for challenging projects, showcase your initiative, and advocate for your career aspirations.

Remember, lifelong learning is key to success in facility management. By actively investing in your skills and building your network, you'll unlock exciting career opportunities and become a valuable asset to any organization.

Bonus Tip:

As you delve into your learning journey, remember that soft skills are just as crucial as technical expertise. Consider incorporating these action items to hone your soft skills:

- **Seek opportunities to improve your communication:** Volunteer for presentations, participate in team-building exercises, or join Toastmasters International.

- **Practice active listening:** Pay close attention to others, ask clarifying questions, and demonstrate empathy.

- **Develop your conflict resolution skills:** Learn to approach disagreements constructively, find common ground, and reach mutually beneficial solutions.

- **Foster collaboration:** Be a team player, share information openly, and encourage participation from all members.

- **Develop your problem-solving skills:** Think critically, analyze situations objectively, and propose creative solutions.

By prioritizing both technical and soft skills, you'll become a well-rounded facility professional equipped to lead with confidence and navigate the dynamic world of facility management.

Chapter 5
From Jack-of-All-Trades to Master:
Discovering Your Passion in Facility Management

Facility management is an orchestra of many instruments, demanding versatility and adaptability. But within this vibrant symphony lies the opportunity to discover your unique melody, become a virtuoso in your chosen area, and contribute to the harmonious functioning of the entire ensemble. This chapter guides you on a journey of self-discovery, helping you identify your passion, hone your skills, and evolve from a versatile player to a true master of your craft.

Why Tune into Your Niche?

While a solid foundation in all aspects of facility management is valuable, specialization offers distinct advantages:

- **Expertise on Autopilot:** Become the go-to resource and trusted advisor in your chosen area, recognized for your in-depth knowledge and practical skills.

- **Market Magnet:** Stand out from the crowd with your specialized skillset, attracting employers seeking experts in high-demand areas like sustainability, technology integration, or security.

- **Earning Potential Unleashed:** Specialized skills often command higher salaries, reflecting the depth of your knowledge and unique value proposition.

- **Intrinsic Reward:** Align your career with your natural inclinations and interests, boosting job satisfaction and professional fulfillment.

Exploring the Diverse Orchestra:

Facility management isn't just about wrenches and screwdrivers, but rather a diverse repertoire of specialized instruments waiting to be mastered. Here are some popular sections where you can find your unique melody:

- **Operations & Maintenance:** Become the conductor of building systems, ensuring smooth daily operations and maximizing equipment lifespan through preventive strategies. Explore resources and courses.

- **Project Management:** Lead the charge for facility transformations, orchestrating projects from inception to completion. Master critical path methods with platforms like Coursera's Project Management Specialization or earn the Project Management Institute (PMI) Certified Project Management (PMP) credential.

- **Space Optimization:** Transform wasted space into vibrant, functional workplaces that support employee well-being and organizational goals. Learn space planning principles with Spatial Management Planning or explore software like SpaceIQ or Archibus.

- **Sustainability Champion:** Be the green knight,

minimizing environmental impact through energy efficiency, waste reduction, and sustainable practices. Earn the LEED AP Building Operations + Maintenance credential or join networks like the US Green Building Council (USGBC).

- **Tech Trailblazer:** Embrace cutting-edge building automation systems, data analytics, and other technologies to optimize performance and efficiency. Upskill with EdX's Introduction to Building Automation Systems course or consider certifications like BACnet Building Operator Certification (BOC).

- **Security Guardian:** Safeguard people and assets, developing robust security protocols, emergency response plans, and business continuity strategies. Pursue the Certified Protection Professional (CPP) designation or explore resources from the American Society for Industrial Security (ASIS).

Finding Your Perfect Harmony:

Choosing your niche involves self-reflection and strategic planning:

- **Strengths & Passions:** What are your natural talents? What excites you within the facility management realm? Consider taking career assessments or exploring industry publications to spark ideas.

- **Future Focus:** Consider industry trends, emerging technologies, and areas with strong job growth potential. Research future-proof skills like data analysis, cyber security, and artificial intelligence.

- **Long-Term Vision:** Does your chosen path align with your career aspirations and leadership goals? Aim for roles that leverage your expertise and challenge you to grow.

- **Mentorship Matters:** Seek guidance from experienced professionals or career counselors to gain valuable insights and perspectives. Network with people in your chosen field and learn from their journeys.

Mastering Your Melody:

Once you've identified your passion, continuous learning and skill development are key:

- **Sharpen Your Skills:** Pursue relevant training and certifications, building industry-recognized credentials that showcase your expertise. Explore the vast array of online courses, professional development programs, and industry conferences available.

- **Network with Peers:** Connect with fellow specialists, share knowledge, learn from their experiences, and stay ahead of the curve. Join professional associations, participate in online forums, and attend industry events.

- **Embrace Challenges:** Seek opportunities that test your skills, broaden your knowledge base, and push you to new levels of expertise. Volunteer for challenging projects, lead initiatives, and contribute to your organization's growth.

- **Stay Informed:** Actively engage with industry publications, attend conferences, and participate in online forums to remain current on trends and best practices. Subscribe to facility management journals, follow thought leaders on social media, and stay curious about the evolving landscape.

Beyond the Solo:

Remember, specialization doesn't mean isolation. Remain a well-rounded facility professional by:

- **Maintaining the Foundation:** Don't neglect core facility management knowledge as it provides a crucial understanding of the bigger picture and fosters collaboration with colleagues from different specialties.

- **Collaboration Catalyst:** Work seamlessly with colleagues from different specialties to achieve shared organizational objectives. Recognize that your expertise complements theirs, creating a harmonious performance within the facility management orchestra.

- **Clear Communication:** Effectively articulate your expertise to non-specialists, fostering collaboration and stakeholder engagement. Translate your technical knowledge into accessible terms and tailor your communication style to different audiences.

Evolving Together:

The world of facility management is constantly evolving, demanding adaptability and continuous learning. Here's how you can stay ahead of the curve:

- **Embrace the Dynamic Duo of Tech & Sustainability:** The integration of technology and sustainability practices is reshaping the field. Master technology to optimize operations and champion sustainable initiatives to contribute to a greener future.

- **Lifelong Learning Ethos:** Embrace the mindset of a lifelong learner. Stay curious, explore new trends, and actively seek opportunities to expand your knowledge and skillset.

- **Be a Changemaker:** Don't wait for change to happen; be the driving force for innovation and improvement. Contribute to industry forums, share your expertise, and inspire others to excel in their chosen areas.

Finding Your Unique Melody:

Finding your niche is a continuous journey, not a static destination. Explore, experiment, and embrace learning along the way. By mastering your chosen craft, you become an invaluable asset, contributing significantly to your organization's success and shaping the future of facility management. Remember, the most beautiful music arises from harmonious collaboration, where diverse instruments join together to create a captivating symphony. So, discover your unique melody, join the orchestra, and play your part in creating a vibrant and thriving facility management landscape.

Bonus Tip: Bringing the Chapter to Life with Real-World Examples and Resources

Inspiring Anecdotes:

- A passionate technician identified recurring energy inefficiencies in their hospital, spearheaded green initiatives after upskilling in energy auditing, and became a recognized Sustainability Manager. This demonstrates the power of passion and continuous learning.

- A dedicated janitor's attention to detail and eagerness to learn led to cross-training opportunities and ultimately a promotion to Operations Manager, showcasing the impact of initiative and commitment on career development.

Expert Insights:
Interview with a CEO of a technology-focused building solutions company:

Interview with a Sustainability Director at a major company:

Practical Resources & Online Platforms:
Operations & Maintenance:
- Resource: Facility Management courses online

- Platform: Building Operating Management magazine

- Online Community: Facility Management Professionals Network

Project Management:
- Resource: Coursera's Project Management Specialization

- Platform: PMI website and forums

- Online Community: Project Management Institute (PMI) Community

Space Optimization:

- Platform: SpaceIQ space planning software

- Online Community: International Facility Management Association (IFMA) Space Committee

Sustainability:

- Resource: LEED AP Building Operations + Maintenance credential

- Platform: US Green Building Council website and events

- Online Community: GreenBiz website and forums

Technology Integration:

- Resource: EdX's Introduction to Building Automation Systems course

- Platform: BACnet International website and resources

- Online Community: Building Automation Control Network (BACnet) International

Security & Emergency Management:

- Resource: Certified Protection Professional (CPP) designation

- Platform: American Society for Industrial Security (ASIS) website and publications

- Online Community: ASIS International online communities

Connect & Engage:
- Encourage readers to join relevant online communities like IFMA, BOMA, and industry-specific groups on professional networking platforms.

- Highlight the value of attending industry conferences and events for networking and staying updated.

- Share links to online forums and social media groups where facility professionals can connect and learn from each other.

Chapter 6
Financial Acumen
Budgeting, Cost Control, and Commercial Awareness

Facility management encompasses more than just keeping the lights on and the doors open. It's about making strategic decisions that maximize efficiency, minimize costs, and ultimately contribute to the organization's financial health. This chapter equips you with the essential financial acumen needed to become a budget wizard, a cost control champion, and a commercially savvy facility professional.

Why Build Your Financial Muscle?

Understanding finances empowers you to:

- **Make informed decisions:** Allocate resources effectively, prioritize projects strategically, and justify investments based on sound financial reasoning.

- **Optimize resource utilization:** Reduce waste, negotiate favorable contracts, and implement cost-saving initiatives, directly impacting the bottom line.

- **Become a valuable asset:** Possessing financial literacy sets you apart, earning recognition as a strategic thinker and contributor to organizational success.

- **Unlock career opportunities:** Advance your career by demonstrating your ability to understand and manage financial aspects of facility operations.

Mastering the Budgetary Balancing Act:
- **Budgeting Essentials:**
  - **Understanding budget types:** Learn the nuances of operating budgets, capital expenditure budgets, and cash flow forecasts.

- **Developing a realistic budget:** Analyze historical data, project future trends, and consider various factors impacting expenditures.

- **Tracking and monitoring:** Regularly monitor budget performance, identify variances, and implement corrective actions as needed.

- **Software Savvy:** Leverage budgeting software and financial modeling tools to streamline the process and gain deeper insights.

- **Communication is Key:** Effectively communicate budget details to stakeholders, justifying allocations and securing buy-in for cost-saving measures.

Cost Control: Your Penny-Pinching Prowess:
- **Procurement Power:**

  - **Negotiation skills:** Hone your negotiation skills to secure the best deals on goods and services for your facility.

  - **Vendor management:** Develop strong relationships with vendors, fostering mutually beneficial partnerships and exploring long-term contracts for cost savings.

- **Competitive sourcing:** Regularly compare prices and seek alternative suppliers to ensure you're getting the best value for your money.

- **Resource Efficiency:**

  - **Energy management:** Implement energy-saving strategies like optimizing lighting, upgrading equipment, and adopting renewable energy sources.

  - **Preventive maintenance:** Prioritize preventive maintenance to minimize costly repairs and equipment downtime.

  - **Waste reduction:** Develop strategies to reduce waste generation in areas like water, paper, and supplies.

Commercial Awareness: Seeing the Bigger Picture:

- **Market Trends:** Stay informed about market trends impacting your industry, such as evolving technology, sustainability regulations, and economic fluctuations.

- **Benchmarking:** Benchmark your facility's performance against industry standards to identify areas for improvement and cost optimization.

- **Understanding the Business:** Gain a broader understanding of your organization's overall business goals and strategic objectives, aligning your facility management practices accordingly.

Beyond the Numbers: The Human Touch

Remember, financial acumen is not just about crunching numbers. It's also about:

- **Building relationships:** Collaborate effectively with finance and other departments to gain insights and achieve shared goals.

- **Effective communication:** Translate financial information into clear and concise terms for non-financial stakeholders.

- **Change management:** Lead by example, fostering a culture of cost-consciousness and resource responsibility within your team.

Investing in Your Financial Future:

Developing financial acumen is a continuous learning journey. Here are some resources to get you started:

- **Professional development courses:** Enroll in courses offered by organizations like IFMA or BOMA on budgeting, cost control, and financial management.

- **Industry publications:** Subscribe to industry publications like Building Operating Management or Facilities Management Journal to stay informed about trends and best practices.

- **Networking opportunities:** Attend industry events and conferences to connect with other professionals and learn from their experiences.

By mastering the financial aspects of facility management, you not only become a valuable asset to your organization but also unlock exciting career opportunities. Remember, every penny saved contributes to the bigger picture, and your financial acumen is the key to unlocking sustainable success for your facility and your career.

Bonus Tip: Unveiling the Power of Financial Acumen in Action

Case Studies: Real-World Impact:

- **Energy Efficiency Transformation:** A hospital implemented a comprehensive energy-saving program, including LED lighting upgrades, smart thermostats, and behavioral change initiatives. This resulted in a 20% reduction in energy costs and significant environmental benefits.

- **Preventive Maintenance Pays Off:** A manufacturing facility adopted a data-driven preventive maintenance program, reducing equipment downtime by 30% and avoiding costly repairs. This saved the company millions of dollars annually.

- **Waste Reduction Revolution:** A large office building launched a waste reduction program, including recycling initiatives, paperless processes, and composting. This initiative diverted tons of waste from landfills and generated cost savings through reduced waste disposal fees.

Industry Data: Quantifying the Advantage:

- A study by McKinsey & Company found that companies with strong financial literacy among their facility management teams achieve cost savings of 10-20% compared to those lacking this expertise.

- A report by the World Green Building Council revealed that investing in energy-efficient green buildings can generate a return on investment of 20-30% through reduced operating costs and increased asset value.

- Research by the Facilities Management Association (FMA) showed that facility professionals with financial acumen are more likely to be promoted to leadership positions within their organizations.

Expert Insights: From the Pros Themselves:

- **Finance Director, Tech Company:** "Understanding financial statements and interpreting data allows facility managers to communicate effectively with executives and secure funding for critical projects."

- **Sustainability Consultant:** "Financial literacy empowers facility managers to identify and implement cost-saving green initiatives that contribute to both environmental and economic sustainability."

- **Chief Operating Officer, Healthcare Facil-**

ity: "Facility professionals with strong financial acumen are essential partners in achieving cost-efficiency and ensuring the financial well-being of our organization."

Here are some real-world best practices, financial equations, and other general modeling techniques that people should learn and explore more:

Real-world best practices:

- **5 Whys:** This problem-solving technique involves asking "why" five times to drill down to the root cause of an issue.

- **SWOT analysis:** This strategic planning tool helps identify strengths, weaknesses, opportunities, and threats to make informed decisions.

- **SMART goals:** Setting Specific, Measurable, Achievable, Relevant, and Time-bound goals ensures clarity and focus.

- **Kanban board:** This visual project management tool helps visualize workflow and manage tasks efficiently.

- **Six Sigma:** This methodology focuses on reducing defects and improving process quality.

- **Lean manufacturing:** This approach eliminates waste and optimizes production processes.

- **Agile methodology:** This flexible approach to project management adapts to changing requirements.

- **Design thinking:** This human-centered approach focuses on understanding user needs and designing solutions that meet them.

- **Growth hacking:** This unconventional marketing strategy uses low-cost and creative methods to achieve rapid growth.

Financial equations:

- **Present Value (PV):** Used to determine the current worth of future cash flows.

- **Future Value (FV):** Used to calculate the future worth of a current investment.

- **Net Present Value (NPV):** Used to assess the profitability of an investment by considering the time value of money.

- **Internal Rate of Return (IRR):** Used to determine the discount rate that makes the NPV of an investment equal to zero.

- **Payback Period:** Used to calculate the time it takes to recover the initial investment.

- **Break-Even Analysis:** Used to determine the point at which sales revenue equals total costs.

- **Capital Expenditure (CapEx):** Used to assess the cost of acquiring or upgrading physical assets.

- **Return on Investment (ROI):** Used to measure the profitability of an investment relative to its cost.

- **Margin**: Used to measure the profitability of a product or service.

- **Key Performance Indicators (KPIs):** Used to track and measure the progress towards strategic goals.

Other general modeling techniques:
- **Data visualization:** Using charts, graphs, and other visual elements to communicate information effectively.

- **Statistical analysis:** Identifying patterns and trends in data to make informed decisions.

- **Scenario planning:** Exploring different possible futures to prepare for contingencies.

- **Decision trees:** Visualizing the potential outcomes of different decisions.

- **Monte Carlo simulation:** Estimating the probability of different outcomes based on random inputs.

- **System dynamics modeling:** Understanding the complex interactions between different parts of a system.

- **Agent-based modeling:** Simulating the behavior of individual agents within a system.

Remember, the specific best practices, equations, and modeling techniques you should learn will depend on your specific field and career goals. However, by focusing on learning how to apply these concepts in real-world situations, you can develop valuable skills that will help you succeed in any field.

Additionally, consider exploring online resources like:

- Coursera: Offers a variety of courses on topics like business analytics, financial modeling, and data science.

- edX: Provides courses on topics like project management, statistics, and machine learning.

- Khan Academy: Offers free courses on a variety of topics, including finance, economics, and statistics.

- Udemy: Provides a wide range of paid and free courses on a variety of topics, including business, design, and technology.

These resources can provide a great starting point for learning new skills and exploring different modeling techniques.

Chapter 7
Contracts and Vendors
Building Strategic Partnerships for Facility Success

The world of facility management thrives on collaboration. While your expertise is invaluable, no single person can manage every aspect of maintaining and optimizing a facility. This is where vendors, your chosen partners, step in. But navigating the intricate world of contracts and vendor relationships requires more than just signing dotted lines. It demands strategic thinking, effective communication, and a focus on building mutually beneficial partnerships.

Why Partner, Not Just Procure?

The traditional buyer-seller dynamic often falls short in facility management. Viewing vendors as strategic partners fosters:

- **Shared Expertise:** Leverage their specialized knowledge and experience to complement your own, tackling complex challenges together.

- **Innovation:** Encourage new ideas and solutions, driving continuous improvement and adaptation within your facility.

- **Cost Optimization:** Negotiate win-win agreements that benefit both parties, leading to cost-effectiveness and long-term value.

- **Risk Mitigation:** Share risks and responsibilities, enhancing overall project success and minimizing potential liabilities.

- **Relationship Building:** Foster trust and collaboration, creating a supportive network of experts for long-term success.

Understanding Your Partner Landscape:

Not all vendors are created equal. Identify the types of partnerships you need based on your facility's unique requirements:

- **Primary Service Providers:** These are crucial partners managing core functions like cleaning, maintenance, and security.

- **Specialist Service Providers:** Engage them for specific needs like pest control, landscaping, or specialized equipment maintenance.

- **Technology & Innovation Partners:** Collaborate with them to implement cutting-edge solutions for automation, energy optimization, or data management.

- **Sustainable Partners:** Seek partners who share your commitment to environmental responsibility and green practices.

Crafting the Foundation: The Art of Contract Negotiation

A well-defined contract establishes expectations and protects both parties. Key elements to focus on:

- **Scope of Work:** Clearly define the services, deliverables, and responsibilities of each party.

- **Performance Standards:** Set measurable standards to assess service quality and ensure agreed-upon outcomes.

- **Payment Terms:** Negotiate fair and transparent payment schedules aligned with deliverables and performance.

- **Termination Clauses:** Outline clear procedures for contract termination under specific circumstances.

- **Dispute Resolution:** Establish a framework for resolving any disagreements amicably and efficiently.

Beyond the Signature: Nurturing a Thriving Partnership

Contracts are just the beginning. Building strong partnerships requires ongoing communication and collaboration:

- **Open Communication:** Maintain regular communication channels, sharing updates, concerns, and feedback openly.

- **Joint Problem-Solving:** Approach challenges collaboratively, seeking mutually beneficial solutions that address both parties' needs.

- **Performance Reviews:** Conduct regular performance reviews to assess progress, identify areas for improvement, and celebrate successes.

- **Relationship Building:** Invest in building personal relationships with key vendor contacts, fostering trust and understanding.

- **Continuous Improvement:** Collaborate on continuous improvement initiatives, optimizing processes and maximizing value for both parties.

Navigating the Digital Age: Technology & Transparency

Technology is transforming the vendor landscape. Consider these advancements:

- **Contract Management Software:** Streamline contract management with electronic document storage, automated reminders, and collaboration tools.

- **Performance Monitoring Platforms:** Utilize real-time data and analytics to track performance against agreed-upon standards and KPIs.

- **Communication & Collaboration Tools:** Leverage online platforms and communication tools to facilitate seamless communication and information sharing.

- **Transparency & Sustainability Partnerships:** Collaborate with vendors who embrace transparency and share data related to sustainability efforts like energy consumption and waste management.

Embrace the Power of Partnership:

By approaching vendor relationships strategically, you move beyond mere transactions and create partnerships that contribute significantly to your facility's success. Remember, it's not just about finding the right vendors, but about creating an ecosystem of collaboration, innovation, and shared goals. By nurturing these partnerships and leveraging technology, you unlock the full potential of your facility, achieving greater efficiency, sustainability, and overall success.

Best Practices, Equations, and Acronyms for Contracts & Vendor Management:

Best Practices:

- **Early and Active Engagement:** Involve procurement, legal, and operational teams early in the vendor selection process to ensure thorough vetting and aligned expectations.

- **Clearly Defined Scope of Work (SOW):** Use clear, concise language in the SOW to avoid ambiguity and disputes. Include detailed descriptions of services, deliverables, timelines, acceptance criteria, and performance metrics.

- **Service Level Agreements (SLAs):** Establish measurable SLAs that outline expected service quality, response times, and consequences for non-compliance.

- **Competitive Bidding:** Encourage competition where feasible to secure the best value proposal and negotiate favorable terms.

- **Transparent Communication:** Maintain open and regular communication with vendors, sharing updates, concerns, and feedback proactively.

- **Regular Performance Reviews:** Conduct periodic performance reviews to assess progress, identify areas for improvement, and celebrate successes.

- **Relationship Building:** Invest in building positive relationships with key vendor contacts, fostering trust, and collaboration.

- **Leverage Technology:** Utilize contract management software, performance monitoring platforms, and communication tools for efficient collaboration and data-driven decision-making.

Financial Equations:

- **Total Cost of Ownership (TCO):** Consider not just the initial price but also ongoing costs like maintenance, training, and consumables when evaluating vendor proposals.

- **Net Present Value (NPV):** Use NPV to compare the present value of different bids, accounting for time value of money and potential long-term costs.

- **Return on Investment (ROI):** Measure the financial benefit of partnering with a particular vendor based on cost savings, improved efficiency, or other benefits.

Acronyms & Standards:

- **SOW:** Scope of Work

- **SLA:** Service Level Agreement

- **KPI:** Key Performance Indicator

- **RFP:** Request for Proposal

- **RFQ:** Request for Quotation

- **TCO:** Total Cost of Ownership

- **NPV:** Net Present Value

- **ROI:** Return on Investment

- **ISO:** International Organization for Standardization (e.g., ISO 9001 for quality management)

- **ASTM:** American Society for Testing and Materials (e.g., ASTM International standards for building materials)

- **LEED:** Leadership in Energy and Environmental Design (green building certification)

Navigating Contract Landmines: Understanding Key Terms and Avoiding Traps

Contracts can be daunting documents, filled with unfamiliar language and potentially hidden clauses. Here's a breakdown of key terms related to liquidated damages and other aspects you should pay attention to:

Liquidated Damages:

- **Meaning:** Agreed-upon compensation paid by a vendor for failing to meet specific contractual obligations, like delayed delivery or unsatisfactory service.

- **Protections:** Clearly define the types of breaches, associated damage amounts, and calculation methods to ensure fairness and avoid disputes.

- **Traps:** Excessively high liquidated damages can be deemed penalties and unenforceable. Seek legal advice to ensure reasonableness and alignment with potential actual damages.

Other Key Terms:

- **Force Majeure:** Clauses outlining events beyond either party's control (natural disasters, strikes) excusing performance obligations. Understand covered events and potential for extended timelines.

- **Indemnification:** Clauses requiring one party to compensate the other for losses or damages arising from their actions or omissions. Negotiate limitations and clarity on covered scenarios.

- **Dispute Resolution:** Mechanisms for resolving disagreements, such as mediation or arbitration. Understand the process, costs, and potential implications.

- **Warranties & Guarantees:** Distinguish between guarantees of specific outcomes and general workmanship assurances. Negotiate limitations and warranty periods.

- **Term & Termination:** Defined contract duration and termination clauses specifying reasons and procedures for ending the agreement. Negotiate fair termination rights for both parties.

- **Confidentiality:** Clauses protecting sensitive information shared during the partnership. Define covered information, permissible uses, and disclosure procedures.

Beyond the Terms:
- **Read the Entire Contract:** Don't rely solely on summaries or verbal promises. Understand every clause and its implications.

- **Seek Professional Help:** For complex contracts or significant value deals, consult legal counsel specializing in contract review and negotiation.

- **Ask Questions:** Don't hesitate to clarify any confusing terms or request changes to ensure alignment with your expectations.

- **Document Communication:** Keep records of all communication and agreements related to the contract, including emails, memos, and meeting minutes.

Seek Legal Counsel:

Consult with an attorney specializing in procurement and contract law when dealing with complex projects, high-value contracts, or potential legal risks.

Additional Resources:

- National Association of State Procurement Officials (NASPO): https://www.naspo.org/

- Institute for Supply Management (ISM): https://www.ismworld.org/

- American Bar Association (ABA) Section of Public Contract Law: https://www.americanbar.org/groups/public_contract_law/

Chapter 8
Navigating Career Progression
Crafting Your Journey in Facility Management

The world of facility management offers a vast landscape for career exploration and growth. From entry-level roles to executive positions, the possibilities are diverse, exciting, and continually evolving. This chapter equips you with the tools and insights to navigate your career journey, chart your unique path, and achieve your professional aspirations.

Self-Discovery: Identifying Your Goals & Strengths

- **Passion & Purpose:** Reflect on what drives you. Do you enjoy hands-on problem-solving, strategic planning, sustainability initiatives, or fostering high-performing teams?

- **Skills & Interests:** Identify your strengths and areas of interest. Are you analytical, detail-oriented, a strong communicator, or a people person?

- **Personality & Values:** What work environment thrives you? Do you prefer autonomy, collaboration, working with diverse teams, or leading others?

Mapping Your Trajectory: Exploring Diverse Paths

- **Specialization:** Deepen your expertise in areas like sustainability, project management, technology integration, or operations & maintenance.

- **Leadership Development:** Develop your leadership skills through courses, mentorships, and taking on project leadership roles.

- **Entrepreneurial Spirit:** Consider branching out to start your own facility management consulting firm or specializing in niche services.

- **Industry Transitions:** Explore opportunities in related fields like real estate, hospitality, healthcare, or education, leveraging your transferable skills.

Fueling Your Ascent: Continuous Learning & Skill Development

- **Formal Education:** Pursue professional certifications like IFMA's CFM credential or specialized degrees in facility management or related fields.

- **Informal Learning:** Attend industry conferences, webinars, and workshops to stay current with trends and technologies.

- **Networking:** Build connections with other facility professionals, mentors, and industry leaders through professional organizations and events.

- **Mentorship:** Seek guidance and advice from experienced mentors who can share insights and support your career development.

Building Your Personal Brand: Marketing Yourself for Success

- **Craft a Compelling Resume:** Highlight your

achievements, skills, and unique value proposition tailored to target positions.

- **Develop a Strong Online Presence:** Build a professional LinkedIn profile showcasing your expertise and industry engagement.

- **Refine Your Communication Skills:** Hone your communication skills, both written and verbal, to effectively articulate your value and career aspirations.

- **Actively Seek Opportunities:** Don't just wait for job postings. Network actively, express your interest to desired companies, and explore diverse avenues for career progression.

Beyond the Conventional: Embracing Unconventional Strategies

- **Volunteer Opportunities:** Offer your expertise to non-profit organizations or community projects, gaining valuable experience and building your network.

- **Internal Mobility:** Explore opportunities within your current organization for promotions, cross-departmental collaborations, or leadership roles.

- **International Experience:** Consider international exposure through internships, projects, or conferences to broaden your perspective and skillset.

- **Entrepreneurial Ventures:** Start a blog, create online courses, or offer consulting services related to your expertise, building your brand and showcasing your thought leadership.

Exploring the Diverse Flavors of Facility Management: Finding Your Perfect Fit

Facility management isn't one-size-fits-all. It's a dynamic field offering a multitude of flavors, each with its unique characteristics and challenges. Understanding your motivations and drivers is key to finding the sub-industry and role that ignites your passion and fuels your career ascent.

Beyond the Stereotypes:

Forget the image of a single role managing an office building. Facility professionals can be found in diverse settings, each bringing their unique expertise to ensure smooth operations and optimal functionality. Here's a glimpse into some exciting possibilities:

- **Thriving in Hospitality:** As a Chief Engineer in a hotel, you'll orchestrate seamless guest experiences, ensuring comfort, safety, and impeccable service through efficient management of building systems, maintenance, and energy consumption.

- **Shaping the Future with Real Estate Developers:** Join a development team and contribute to groundbreaking projects. Your expertise in sustainable design, space optimization, and efficient construction practices will shape the built environment of tomorrow.

- **Innovating in the High-Tech Arena:** Working in a fast-paced tech environment demands agility and adaptability. You'll manage cutting-edge facilities, ensuring reliability, security, and support for the ever-evolving needs of technology companies.

- **Retail Dynamism:** Keep retail spaces vibrant and operational as a Facility Manager. From maintaining seamless customer experiences to optimizing energy use and ensuring compliance, you'll play a crucial role in the retail industry's success.

- **Healthcare Hero:** In hospitals and healthcare facilities, your expertise translates into patient well-being. You'll oversee sterile environments, ensure life-saving equipment functions flawlessly, and prioritize patient safety and comfort.

- **Manufacturing Maestro:** As a Plant Manager, you'll lead the symphony of production. Efficient facility operations, preventive maintenance, and optimizing energy use are your keys to ensuring smooth manufacturing processes and contributing to the company's bottom line.

Matching Your Passions to Your Path:

This is just a taste of the diverse roles and industries waiting to be explored. The key lies in uncovering what truly motivates you:

- **Do you thrive in fast-paced, dynamic environments like the tech industry?**

- **Does meticulous attention to detail and ensuring guest comfort resonate with your hos-**

pitality spirit?

- **Are you passionate about sustainability and shaping the future of building practices?**

- **Does ensuring the smooth operation of complex systems in healthcare settings appeal to your problem-solving abilities?**

- **Does contributing to the efficiency and success of manufacturing processes excite you?**

By aligning your passions with the unique characteristics of each sub-industry, you can discover the flavor of facility management that perfectly satisfies your professional appetite.

Remember, your career journey is a continuous exploration. Once you start exploring the diverse flavors of facility management, you'll find a path that not only aligns with your skills and interests but also ignites your passion and fuels your professional growth.

From Facility Management to Workspace Wizards: The Rise of REWS and Beyond

The world of work is undergoing a dynamic transformation, and so is the role of facility management. What was once primarily focused on maintaining the physical building is now evolving into a strategic function impacting employee experience, business performance, and organizational success. This evolution has given rise to new terms and titles, including Workspace Management and the latest buzzword: Real Estate Workspace Strategy (REWS).

So, what's the difference? It's more than just semantics. The shift signifies a move beyond simply managing facilities to strategically shaping workspaces that support innovation, collaboration, and employee well-being. REWS teams take a holistic approach, integrating facility management with real estate strategy, space planning, technology integration, and human resource considerations.

How Times Have Changed:

- **From Reactive to Proactive:** Gone are the days of solely responding to maintenance issues. Today's workspace managers proactively anticipate needs, analyze data, and design spaces that support evolving workstyles and business objectives.

- **Beyond Bricks and Mortar:** The focus extends beyond physical infrastructure. Technology integration, employee experience design, and sustainability initiatives are integral components of modern workspace management.

- **Data-Driven Decisions:** Intuition is no longer enough. REWS teams leverage data analytics to understand space utilization, employee preferences, and organizational needs, driving evidence-based decisions for optimization and cost-effectiveness.

- **People-Centric Approach:** The human element is paramount. REWS teams prioritize occupant well-being, fostering a healthy, productive, and engaging work environment that attracts and retains top talent.

Anything Within the Building Envelope:
With this evolving landscape, the possibilities for specialization within workspace management are limitless. You can carve your niche, focusing on areas like:

- **Workplace Technology:** Integrate cutting-edge solutions like smart building systems, collaboration tools, and occupancy sensors to optimize space utilization and enhance user experience.

- **Sustainability:** Champion green initiatives, implement energy-efficient practices, and design sustainable workspaces that contribute to environmental responsibility.

- **Change Management:** Guide teams through transitions associated with space changes, ensuring seamless adoption and maximizing the benefits of new work environments.

- **Data Analytics:** Analyze space utilization data, employee feedback, and environmental metrics to identify trends, generate insights, and inform strategic decision-making.

- **Space Planning & Design:** Design flexible, adaptable workspaces that cater to diverse workstyles, foster collaboration, and promote employee well-being.

Remember, the role of workspace management is no longer confined to bricks and mortar. It's about creating inspiring, efficient, and data-driven environments that empower people and fuel organizational success. This exciting field offers limitless opportunities for specialization, continuous learning,

and building a fulfilling career that shapes the future of work.

Action Items: Take Charge of Your Workspace Journey

Now that you've explored the evolving landscape of facility management and workspace creation, here are some action items to turn your newfound knowledge into action:

Self-Discovery:

- **Reflect on your passions and strengths:** What excites you about the different flavors of workspace management? Do you enjoy analyzing data, designing spaces, or implementing technology?

- **Assess your transferable skills:** Identify skills like communication, problem-solving, and project management that are valuable across different areas of this field.

- **Research and explore:** Dive deeper into sub-industries that resonate with you. Learn about the unique challenges and opportunities within each sector.

Skill Development:

- **Seek relevant certifications:** Consider pursuing certifications or the WELL Building Standard Associate (WELL AP) to enhance your expertise.

- **Expand your knowledge base:** Take online courses, attend industry conferences, and network with professionals to stay updated on trends and best practices.

- **Develop specialized skills:** Depending on your chosen path, focus on areas like data analytics, space planning, technology integration, or sustainability.

Career Exploration:

- **Connect with REWS professionals:** Network with people working in this field to gain insights into their daily tasks, challenges, and career paths.

- **Explore job opportunities:** Start searching for roles that align with your interests and skills. Consider both traditional facility management positions and REWS-specific titles.

- **Create a personalized career plan:** Set clear goals and outline steps you'll take to achieve your desired career trajectory.

Remember, this is an ongoing journey. Be proactive, embrace continuous learning, and don't be afraid to explore different opportunities. The ever-evolving world of workspace management offers a fulfilling and rewarding career path for those who are passionate about shaping the future of work.

Chapter 9
Leadership Essentials
From Technician to Coach, Motivating and Guiding Your Team

The world of facility management thrives on collaboration. As you progress in your career, your role transitions from a hands-on technician to a leader, responsible for guiding and motivating a team towards achieving shared goals. This chapter equips you with the essential leadership skills to navigate this transition, build a high-performing team, and cultivate a positive and productive work environment.

Shifting Your Mindset: From Doing to Empowering

- **Recognize the Transformation:** Acknowledge your transition from individual contributor to leader. Your primary focus shifts from technical expertise to people development and team performance.

- **Embrace Empowerment:** Delegate tasks effectively, trust your team members, and create opportunities for them to learn, grow, and take ownership.

- **Foster Collaboration:** Encourage open communication, information sharing, and teamwork to harness the collective strengths of your team.

Key Leadership Competencies:

- **Communication:** Master clear, concise, and two-way communication. Share goals, provide feedback, and actively listen to understand your team's needs and concerns.

- **Motivation:** Inspire and energize your team. Recognize achievements, celebrate successes, and create a motivating work environment that fosters engagement.

- **Conflict Resolution:** Address disagreements

constructively, facilitate respectful dialogue, and find solutions that benefit both individuals and the team.

- **Problem-Solving:** Equip your team to solve problems collaboratively. Guide them through challenges, encourage out-of-the-box thinking, and celebrate innovative solutions.

- **Coaching & Development:** Invest in your team's growth. Provide coaching opportunities, offer training and development programs, and set clear expectations for continuous improvement.

Building a High-Performing Team:

- **Define Shared Goals:** Establish clear, measurable, and achievable goals aligned with the overall organizational objectives. Communicate these goals effectively to your team and foster a sense of shared purpose.

- **Embrace Diversity:** Value individual differences and perspectives. Build a team with diverse skills, backgrounds, and experiences to generate a richer pool of ideas and solutions.

- **Delegate Effectively:** Match tasks with individual strengths and development needs. Provide clear instructions, offer support, and trust your team to deliver.

- **Recognize & Reward:** Acknowledge and celebrate individual and team achievements. Implement a reward system that aligns with desired behaviors and motivates high performance.

- **Provide Feedback:** Offer constructive feedback regularly, focusing on both strengths and areas for improvement. Create a culture of open feedback that facilitates development and growth.

Leading Through Change:

- **Communicate Transparently:** Clearly explain the rationale and objectives behind changes. Address concerns honestly and openly, and encourage two-way communication.

- **Engage Your Team:** Involve your team in the change process whenever possible. Seek their input, encourage active participation, and address their concerns proactively.

- **Focus on Benefits:** Highlight the positive impacts of the change, both for the organization and individuals. Emphasize opportunities for learning, growth, and improvement.

- **Offer Support:** Recognize that change can be challenging. Provide resources, training, and support to help your team adapt and thrive in the new environment.

Remember, effective leadership is a journey, not a destination. Cultivate your leadership skills continuously, invest in your team's development, and foster a positive and collaborative work environment. By doing so, you can motivate your team to achieve exceptional results and empower them to reach their full potential.

Real-Life Leadership Examples:

- A hospital Director of Facilities faced increasing patient flow and limited resources. They formed a cross-functional team to streamline cleaning protocols, fostering open communication, shared goals, and empowerment. The team reduced cleaning time by 20%, improving patient care and staff efficiency.

- A Chief Engineer at a high-tech company recognized the need for agility. They fostered a culture of continuous learning and innovation, encouraging experimentation, providing skill development resources, and celebrating creative solutions. This enabled their team to adapt quickly to changing technology demands.

- A Facility Manager at a large retail chain implemented flexible work arrangements, ergonomic workstations, and wellness programs, demonstrating commitment to employee well-being. Their focus on engagement and a supportive environment resulted in reduced absenteeism, higher productivity, and increased employee satisfaction.

Practical Tools and Resources:
- **Communication Templates:**

  - Weekly team meeting agenda template

  - One-on-one feedback template

  - Recognition and appreciation communication templates

- **Performance Evaluation Frameworks:**

- SMART goals framework
- 360-degree feedback tool
- Performance review template

- **Team-Building Exercises:**

  - Icebreaker activities
  - Collaborative problem-solving exercises
  - Team scavenger hunts
  - Role-playing scenarios

Inspiring Stories of Success:

- A Facility Management team faced budget constraints. They collaborated to identify cost-saving opportunities, proposing innovative solutions and renegotiating contracts, saving 15% on their operational budget. This demonstrates the power of teamwork and creative problem-solving.

- A maintenance team in a multi-unit residential building struggled with long response times and resident complaints. By implementing a preventive maintenance program, improving communication, and fostering a service-oriented attitude, they significantly reduced repair times and increased resident satisfaction scores.

- A diverse team comprised of engineers, energy specialists, and finance professionals collaborated to develop and implement a comprehensive sustainability plan. By leveraging diverse perspectives and skills, they reduced energy consumption by 20% and established the company as a leader in environmental responsibility.

Remember, leadership is not about giving orders; it's about empowering others. These real-life examples, practical tools, and inspiring stories equip aspiring facility management leaders with the knowledge, skills, and resources they need to motivate and guide their teams towards success and shaping the future of the industry.

Chapter 10
Operations and Maintenance
Ensuring Smooth Sailing with Efficient Systems

The heart of any successful facility lies in its **operations and maintenance (O&M)** practices. Just like a well-maintained ship navigates choppy waters with ease, efficient O&M ensures your facility runs smoothly, efficiently, and cost-effectively, supporting your core business objectives. This chapter delves into the essential elements of O&M, equipping you with the knowledge and strategies to optimize your facility's performance and contribute to its long-term success.

Understanding the O&M Landscape:

- **Preventive vs. Reactive:** Proactive preventative

maintenance, like regular inspections and scheduled servicing, prevents costly breakdowns and equipment failures, ultimately saving time and money compared to reactive repairs.

- **Predictive Maintenance:** Leverage technology to predict equipment issues before they occur, minimizing downtime and maximizing equipment lifespan.

- **Data-Driven Decisions:** Utilize data from condition monitoring systems and building management platforms to identify trends, optimize maintenance schedules, and make informed decisions.

Core Components of Effective O&M:

- **Maintenance Management:** Implement a robust maintenance management program that includes procedures, schedules, inventory control, and performance tracking.

- **Workforce Development:** Invest in training and upskilling your maintenance team to ensure they possess the necessary skills and knowledge to handle diverse tasks and emerging technologies.

- **Sustainability Integration:** Prioritize sustainable practices in your O&M procedures, optimizing energy efficiency, minimizing waste, and adopting environmentally friendly solutions.

- **Emergency Preparedness:** Develop and regularly practice emergency response plans for various scenarios, ensuring the safety and well-being of occupants and minimizing potential damage.

Navigating the Digital Age:
- **Building automation systems:** Integrate building automation systems (BAS) to automate tasks, monitor performance in real-time, and optimize energy consumption.

- **Internet of Things (IoT):** Leverage IoT sensors and devices to collect data, gain insights into equipment health, and predict potential issues before they escalate.

- **Big data analytics:** Utilize big data analytics to analyze maintenance data, identify trends, and make data-driven decisions for enhanced efficiency and cost savings.

Optimizing for Success:

- **Benchmarking:** Benchmark your O&M performance against industry standards and best practices to identify areas for improvement.

- **Continuous Improvement:** Embrace a culture of continuous improvement through ongoing evaluation, learning, and implementation of best practices.

- **Collaboration:** Foster collaboration between operations, maintenance, and other departments to ensure aligned goals and efficient communication.

Remember, effective O&M is not a standalone function; it's an integral part of your overall facility management strategy. By implementing the principles and strategies outlined in this chapter, you can ensure your facility operates smoothly, efficiently, and sustainably, contributing to its success and creating a positive experience for occupants and stakeholders.

Real-World Success Stories:

Case Study 1: Hospital Leverages Predictive Maintenance:

A major hospital faced rising equipment repair costs and unplanned downtime. They implemented a predictive maintenance program, utilizing sensor data and analytics to anticipate equipment failures. This approach reduced reactive repairs by 30%, lowered maintenance costs by 15%, and improved equipment uptime, ensuring uninterrupted patient care.

Case Study 2: Retail Giant Optimizes Energy Efficiency:

A large retail chain adopted smart building technology and data analytics to monitor energy consumption across their stores. By optimizing HVAC systems, lighting, and equipment usage based on real-time data, they achieved a 20% reduction in energy costs and significantly lowered their carbon footprint, demonstrating the environmental benefits of efficient O&M.

Cost-Saving Benefits:

- **Reduced downtime and equipment failures:** Proactive maintenance prevents costly repairs and extends equipment lifespan, leading to significant cost savings over time.

- **Improved energy efficiency:** Optimizing building systems and adopting sustainable practices can drastically reduce energy costs and utility bills.

- **Enhanced productivity:** Smoothly operating

facilities with minimal disruptions contribute to increased staff productivity and overall operational efficiency.

Sustainability Impacts:

- **Reduced energy consumption:** Efficient O&M minimizes energy waste, lowering carbon emissions and contributing to environmental sustainability.

- **Minimized waste:** Implementing sustainable practices, such as water conservation and responsible waste management, reduces environmental impact.

- **Improved indoor air quality:** Proper maintenance of HVAC systems ensures optimal air quality, contributing to occupant health and well-being.

Insights from the Pros:
Interview with O&M Manager:
"The key to successful O&M is **prioritization and collaboration**. We prioritize preventive maintenance and leverage data to make informed decisions. Additionally, collaboration between our team, operations, and oth-

er departments is crucial for aligning goals and ensuring smooth system operation."

Interview with Sustainability Specialist:

"Integrating sustainability into O&M practices isn't just about the environment; it's about cost savings too. By optimizing energy efficiency and reducing waste, we achieve both financial and environmental benefits, creating a win-win situation."

Remember, effective O&M is a journey, not a destination. By continuously learning, embracing new technologies, and prioritizing both efficiency and sustainability, you can ensure your facility operates smoothly, minimizes environmental impact, and contributes to the success of your organization.

Bonus Section: Dive Deeper & Take Action!

Key Terms:

- **Preventive Maintenance:** Planned maintenance tasks performed regularly to prevent equipment failures.

- **Predictive Maintenance:** Utilizing data and technology to predict potential equipment issues before they occur.

- **Building Automation Systems (BAS):** Computerized systems that automate building functions like HVAC, lighting, and security.

- **Internet of Things (IoT):** Network of interconnected devices collecting and sharing data to monitor and optimize system performance.

- **Big Data Analytics:** Analyzing large datasets to identify trends, patterns, and insights for informed decision-making.

- **Benchmarking:** Comparing your O&M performance against industry standards to identify areas for improvement.

- **Continuous Improvement:** Ongoing process of evaluating, learning, and implementing best practices to enhance O&M effectiveness.

Action Items:

- **Assess your current O&M practices:** Evaluate your maintenance schedules, preventative measures, and data utilization. Identify areas for improvement and prioritize actions.

- **Explore predictive maintenance op-

tions: Consider implementing sensor-based monitoring or data analytics tools to predict potential equipment failures.

- **Investigate building automation systems:** Research BAS solutions and assess their potential to optimize building operations and energy efficiency.

- **Embrace data-driven decision-making:** Start collecting and analyzing data from your facilities to identify trends and optimize maintenance strategies.

- **Benchmark your performance:** Compare your O&M metrics against industry best practices to identify areas for improvement.

- **Develop a continuous improvement plan:** Establish a plan for evaluating, learning, and implementing best practices to continuously enhance your O&M effectiveness.

- **Network with O&M professionals:** Connect with industry peers through online communities, conferences, or professional organizations to share experiences and learn from each other.

- **Stay informed about advancements:** Keep up-to-date with the latest trends and technologies in O&M through industry publications, webinars, and educational resources.

Remember, by taking action and continuously improving your O&M practices, you can contribute to a more efficient, sustainable, and cost-effective facility operation.

Chapter 11
Tenant and Occupant Relations:
Building Positive Relationships and Fostering a Thriving Community

He success of any facility hinges not just on efficient operations but also on fostering positive relationships with the individuals who inhabit it. Whether tenants, residents, or employees, their experience shapes the overall atmosphere and contributes to the facility's reputation. This chapter delves into the essential principles of building strong tenant and occupant relations, equipping you with strategies to cultivate a thriving community and maximize satisfaction.

Understanding Different Perspectives:

- **Tenants:** Recognize tenants as partners, valuing their needs and concerns. Understand their lease agreements, expectations, and communication preferences.

- **Occupants:** Acknowledge the diverse needs of occupants who may not be directly involved in lease agreements, such as employees, guests, or residents in multi-unit buildings.

- **Community Mindset:** Foster a sense of community where occupants feel valued, connected, and responsible for contributing to a positive environment.

Building Strong Relationships:

- **Clear Communication:** Establish clear communication channels, respond promptly to inquiries, and keep tenants and occupants informed about important updates and changes.

- **Transparency and Trust:** Be transparent in your communication, build trust by honoring commitments, and be fair and consistent in decision-making.

- **Active Listening:** Actively listen to concerns, feedback, and suggestions, demonstrating that you value their input and perspectives.

- **Conflict Resolution:** Address conflicts promptly and professionally, seeking mutually agreeable solutions and fostering a culture of respect and understanding.

Fostering a Thriving Community:

- **Events and Activities:** Organize events and activities that build connections, promote engagement, and foster a sense of belonging and community spirit.

- **Amenities and Services:** Offer amenities and services that cater to the diverse needs and interests of your tenants and occupants, enhancing their overall experience.

- **Feedback Mechanisms:** Establish feedback mechanisms like surveys, suggestion boxes, or open forums to gather valuable input and continuously improve tenant and occupant experience.

- **Recognition and Appreciation:** Recognize and appreciate positive contributions, showing you value their presence and engagement within the community.

Leveraging Technology:

- **Communication Platforms:** Utilize online portals, tenant apps, or communication platforms to share information, facilitate communication, and offer convenient services.

- **Maintenance Management Systems:** Implement online maintenance request systems, allowing tenants and occupants to submit requests easily and track their progress.

- **Virtual Communities:** Foster online communities where tenants and occupants can connect, share information, and build relationships virtually.

Real-World Success Stories:

Case Study 1: Engaging Residents in Sustainability: An apartment complex implemented a resident composting program with educational workshops and community gardens. This initiative not only promoted sustainability but also fostered resident engagement and a sense of community.

Case Study 2: Building Connections Through Events: A co-working space organized regular networking events, workshops, and social gatherings. These events helped tenants connect, build relationships, and create a vibrant community atmosphere.

Insights from the Pros:

Property Manager: "Open communication is key. We hold regular town hall meetings, respond promptly to emails, and actively listen to concerns. This builds trust and fosters a sense of partnership with our tenants."

Facility Director: "We offer diverse amenities like fitness centers, game rooms, and outdoor spaces. By catering to various interests, we create a place where occupants feel comfortable and connected."

Testimonials:

"This community feels like home, not just an apartment building. The events and friendly atmosphere make it a great place to live." - Resident of an apartment complex.

"The co-working space provides a supportive and collaborative environment. I've made valuable connections and grown my business thanks to the community events." - Tenant of a co-working space.

Remember, building strong tenant and occupant relations is an ongoing process. By implementing these strategies, you can cultivate a positive and thriving community, contribute to increased tenant satisfaction and retention, and create a space where individuals feel valued, connected, and engaged.

Bonus Section:

Action Items:

- Assess your current communication channels and feedback mechanisms.

- Identify opportunities to organize community events and offer relevant amenities.

- Explore technology tools to enhance communication and service delivery.

- Develop a plan for gathering and responding to tenant and occupant feedback.

- Recognize and appreciate positive contributions within the community.

Common Terms:

- Tenant: An individual or organization that leases space within a facility.

- Occupant: Someone who physically inhabits a space within a facility, may or may not be a tenant.

- Community Engagement: Activities and initiatives that encourage communication, collaboration, and a sense of belonging among occupants.

- Amenity: A service or feature offered within a facility to enhance the occupant experience.

- **HOA (Homeowners Association):** A non-profit organization responsible for managing a community of individual homeowners, often in shared-ownership situations like condominiums or townhouses.

- **Reserve Study:** A financial analysis that estimates the future repair and replacement costs of major building systems and components, enabling proactive planning and budgeting for capital expenditures.

- **Tenant Turnover:** The rate at which tenants vacate their units and new tenants move in, impacting rental income and overall occupancy levels.

- **Security Deposit:** A refundable deposit collected from tenants to cover potential damages beyond normal wear and tear.

- **Lease Agreement:** A legal contract outlining the terms and conditions of tenancy, including rent amount, duration, tenant responsibilities, and landlord obligations.

- **Maintenance Request:** A formal request from a tenant or occupant to address a repair or service issue within the facility.

- **Amenities:** Services and features offered within a facility to enhance the occupant experience, such as fitness centers, laundry facilities, or swimming pools.

- **Accessibility:** Ensuring the facility is accessible and usable by individuals with disabilities, complying with relevant regulations and promoting inclusivity.

- **Sustainability:** Implementing practices that minimize environmental impact and resource consumption while creating a healthy and comfortable environment for occupants.

- **Smart Building Technology:** Utilizing interconnected sensors, data analytics, and automation to optimize building systems, improve efficiency, and enhance occupant comfort.

- **Co-working Space:** A shared workspace designed for independent professionals and entrepreneurs, offering flexible workspaces, collaborative areas, and networking opportunities.

- **Resident Engagement:** Activities and initiatives aimed at fostering a sense of community and encouraging participation among residents within a multi-unit building.

FAQs:

- How often should I communicate with tenants and occupants?

- What types of events and activities are most effective for building community?

- How can I leverage technology to improve tenant and occupant relations?

Technology can significantly improve communication, engagement, and service delivery:

- **Resident/Tenant Portals:** Provide a central hub for rent payments, maintenance requests, communication, document storage, and community updates.

- **Mobile Apps:** Offer convenient access to building information, amenities booking, event registration, and communication features.

- **Social Media Groups:** Foster virtual communities where residents can connect, share information, and build relationships.

- **Online Feedback Surveys:** Gather valuable insights and suggestions for improvement.

- **Virtual Events:** Host webinars, workshops, and social gatherings online to connect with geographically dispersed occupants.

- How can I handle difficult conversations with tenants or occupants?

- Approach conflicts with professionalism, empathy, and active listening.

- Clearly communicate policies and expectations.

- Seek mutually agreeable solutions that address concerns fairly.

- Maintain a calm and respectful demeanor throughout the interaction.

- Consider involving additional resources or mediation if necessary.

- How can I measure the success of my tenant and occupant relations initiatives?

- Track key metrics like tenant satisfaction surveys, lease renewal rates, maintenance request response times, and event attendance.

- Collect qualitative feedback through surveys, focus groups, and open forums.

- Monitor social media sentiment and online reviews.

- Compare your performance to industry benchmarks and best practices.

Remember, fostering positive tenant and occupant relations is an investment with significant returns. By prioritizing clear communication, transparency, engagement, and a commitment to continuous improvement, you can create a thriving community that attracts and retains occupants, enhances their experience, and contributes to the overall success of your facility.

Additional Resources:

- Building Owners and Managers Association (BOMA): https://www.boma.org/

- National Apartment Association (NAA): https://naant.org/dashboard/

- International WELL Building Institute (IWBI): https://www.wellcertified.com/

Chapter 12
Environmental Stewardship:
Leading the Way in Sustainability

In today's world, prioritizing sustainability is no longer optional for responsible facility management. It's not just about environmental responsibility; it's about cost savings, resource efficiency, and creating a healthier, more comfortable environment for occupants. This chapter delves into the core principles of environmental stewardship, equipping you with the strategies and tools to lead the way in sustainable facility operations.

Understanding Sustainability:

- **Holistic Approach:** Sustainability encompasses environmental, social, and economic considerations, ensuring responsible resource use, minimizing environmental impact, and fostering social equity.

- **Triple Bottom Line:** Consider not just financial profit, but also social and environmental impact when making decisions.

- **Long-Term Perspective:** Implement practices with long-term benefits for the environment, community, and financial well-being of the facility.

Core Strategies for Sustainability:
- **Energy Efficiency:** Optimize building systems, utilize renewable energy sources, and implement energy-saving practices to reduce energy consumption.

- **Water Conservation:** Implement water-efficient fixtures, practices, and landscaping to minimize water usage.

- **Waste Reduction:** Minimize waste generation through recycling, composting, and responsible purchasing practices.

- **Indoor Air Quality:** Ensure optimal indoor air quality through proper ventilation, filtration, and pollutant control measures.

- **Sustainable Materials:** Use environmentally friendly building materials and products whenever possible.

- **Sustainable Transportation:** Encourage alternative transportation options like cycling, walking, or public transit, and optimize fleet efficiency for vehicles.

Leading the Way:

- **Set Sustainability Goals:** Establish measurable and achievable sustainability goals aligned with your organization's values and the facility's needs.

- **Develop a Sustainability Plan:** Create a comprehensive plan outlining specific actions, timelines, and responsible parties for achieving your goals.

- **Engage Stakeholders:** Involve tenants, occupants, employees, and other stakeholders in your sustainability initiatives to foster a collaborative and supportive environment.

- **Track Progress and Measure Results:** Monitor your progress towards sustainability goals, collect data, and measure the impact of your initiatives to demonstrate success and identify areas for improvement.

- **Communicate and Celebrate:** Share your sustainability efforts and achievements with stakeholders, celebrate successes, and inspire others to join your journey.

Leveraging Technology:

- **Building Automation Systems (BAS):** Utilize BAS to optimize energy use, monitor building performance, and automate sustainable practices.

- **Smart Technologies:** Implement smart thermostats, lighting systems, and water management solutions for increased efficiency and data-driven decision-making.

- **Data Analytics:** Analyze energy, water, and waste data to identify trends, optimize performance, and track progress towards goals.

Real-World Examples:

- **Case Study 1: Green Office Building:** A corporate office building implemented energy-efficient systems, renewable energy sources, and water conservation measures, achieving a 30% reduction in energy and water use.

- **Case Study 2: Sustainable Community Garden:** A multi-unit residential complex established a community garden, promoting local food production, waste reduction, and resident engagement.

Insights from Sustainability Leaders:

- **Facility Manager:** "Our sustainability efforts go beyond environmental benefits. They also contribute to cost savings, employee well-being, and attract environmentally conscious tenants."

- **Sustainability Consultant:** "Start small, celebrate successes, and continuously improve. Sustainability is a journey, not a destination."

Remember, even small steps towards sustainability can make a significant impact. By implementing the strategies and tools outlined in this chapter, you can lead the way in environmental stewardship, create a more sustainable future for your facility, and contribute to a healthier planet.

Bonus Section:

Action Items:

- Conduct an environmental audit to assess your facility's current energy, water, and waste footprint.

- Set achievable sustainability goals and develop a plan to achieve them.

- Implement energy-saving measures and promote sustainable practices among occupants.

- Partner with sustainability organizations or consultants to access expertise and resources.

- Track your progress and share your achievements with stakeholders.

Common Terms:

- **Carbon Footprint:** The total amount of greenhouse gases emitted by an individual, organization, or activity.

- **Renewable Energy:** Energy generated from sources that naturally replenish, like solar, wind, or geothermal.

- **Life Cycle Assessment (LCA):** Analyzing the environmental impact of a product or service throughout its entire lifespan.

- **Green Building Certification:** Programs like LEED or WELL Building Standard recognize facilities that meet sustainability criteria.

- **Circular Economy:** A model that minimizes waste and maximizes resource reuse and recycling.

FAQs:

- What are some cost-effective ways to improve sustainability in my facility?

- How can I encourage tenants and occupants to participate in sustainability initiatives?

- What resources are available to help me implement sustainable practices?

Chapter 13
Technology and Automation
Embracing Innovation for Enhanced Efficiency

In today's rapidly evolving landscape, facility management is experiencing a transformative wave driven by technology and automation. From streamlining operations to optimizing resource utilization, embracing these advancements is no longer optional; it's essential for enhancing efficiency, reducing costs, and improving occupant experience. This chapter delves into the exciting world of technology and automation, equipping you with the knowledge and strategies to navigate this digital revolution and unlock its full potential for your facility.

Understanding the Technology Landscape:

- **Internet of Things (IoT):** A network of interconnected devices collecting and sharing data, providing real-time insights into building systems and occupant behavior.

- **Building Automation Systems (BAS):** Integrated systems controlling various building functions like HVAC, lighting, and security, enabling automation and optimized performance.

- **Artificial Intelligence (AI):** Utilizing AI algorithms to analyze data, identify patterns, and automate decision-making processes within the facility.

- **Big Data Analytics:** Collecting and analyzing large datasets to gain insights, optimize operations, and predict future needs.

- **Digital Twins:** Creating virtual replicas of your facility to simulate scenarios, test solutions, and optimize performance before implementation.

Embracing Automation:

- **Automated Maintenance:** Utilize sensor-based monitoring and automated systems to detect and address potential issues before they escalate, reducing downtime and maintenance costs.

- **Smart Access Control:** Implement access control systems with keyless entry, mobile credentials, and biometric authentication for enhanced security and convenience.

- **Automated Waste Management:** Utilize smart bins and waste management systems for efficient collection, data-driven route optimization, and potential waste reduction.

- **Automated Lighting Systems:** Implement sensor-based lighting systems that adapt to occupancy and natural light, reducing energy consumption.

- **Robotic Cleaning:** Introduce robots for repetitive cleaning tasks, freeing up staff for more complex tasks and enhancing cleaning efficiency.

Optimizing for Success:
- **Identify Automation Opportunities:** Conduct a comprehensive assessment of your facility operations to identify areas where automation can bring significant benefit.

- **Prioritize and Plan:** Prioritize automation projects based on potential impact, ease of implementation, and budget constraints. Develop detailed plans with clear objectives, timelines, and responsible parties.

- **Change Management:** Prepare occupants and staff for automation by providing clear communication, training, and addressing potential concerns.

- **Data-Driven Decisions:** Integrate data analytics into your decision-making process to ensure chosen technologies align with your goals and measure the impact of automation on key performance indicators.

- **Security and Privacy:** Implement robust cybersecurity measures and ensure data privacy compliance when deploying new technologies.

Real-World Success Stories:
- **Case Study 1: Smart Hospital Operations:** A hospital implemented an IoT-based system to monitor equipment health, automate maintenance tasks, and optimize energy consump-

tion, leading to significant cost savings and improved patient care.

- **Case Study 2: Automated Retail Facility:** A retail store adopted robotic systems for inventory management and warehouse operations, resulting in increased efficiency, reduced errors, and improved product availability.

Insights from Technology Leaders:

- **Facility Director:** "Technology isn't a replacement for our staff; it's an empowering tool. Automation frees them up for higher-value tasks and improves overall operational efficiency."

- **Technology Consultant:** "Start small, learn, and adapt. Technology changes rapidly, so embrace a flexible approach and continuously evaluate new solutions."

Remember, technology and automation are not simply tools; they are strategic enablers. By carefully choosing and implementing the right solutions, you can unlock significant benefits for your facility, from enhanced efficiency and cost savings to improved occupant experience and a more sustainable future.

Action Items:

- Conduct an assessment of your current technology infrastructure and identify potential automation opportunities.

- Explore and research available technology solutions aligned with your needs and budget.

- Develop a strategic plan for technology implementation, considering your goals, stakeholders, and budget.

- Partner with technology providers and consultants to access expertise and ensure successful implementation.

- Educate your staff and occupants about the benefits of technology and automation.

Common Terms:

- **Cloud Computing:** Storing and accessing data and applications over the internet instead of local servers.

- **Cybersecurity:** Protecting your facility's digital systems and data from unauthorized access, use, disclosure, disruption, modification, or destruction.

- **Machine Learning:** Utilizing algorithms that learn and improve from data without explicit programming.

- **Blockchain:** A distributed ledger technology ensuring secure and transparent data sharing.

- **Digital Signage:** Utilizing electronic displays for communication, information sharing, and advertising within the facility.

FAQs:

- What are the security risks associated with technology and automation?

- How can I ensure smooth adoption and minimize disruption when implementing new technologies?

- What resources are available to help me navigate the technology landscape and make informed decisions?

Understanding the Key Players:

- **CMMS:** Software designed to manage maintenance activities, including work orders, scheduling, inventory, preventive maintenance tasks, and reporting.

- **BAS:** Integrated systems controlling various building functions like HVAC, lighting, and security, collecting real-time data on equipment performance and environmental conditions.

Unveiling the Benefits of Integration:

- **Predictive Maintenance:** Combine BAS sensor data with CMMS historical data to predict equipment failures, enabling proactive maintenance and preventing costly downtime.

- **Reduced Maintenance Costs:** Optimize maintenance schedules and resource allocation based on real-time equipment health insights, minimizing reactive repairs and unnecessary interventions.

- **Improved Operational Efficiency:** Automate work order generation based on BAS alerts, streamlining communication and response times for maintenance teams.

- **Enhanced Data-Driven Decision Mak-

ing: Leverage combined data from CMMS and BAS to identify trends, analyze energy consumption, and optimize system performance across the facility.

- **Extended Equipment Lifespan:** Implement preventive maintenance based on real-time equipment data, preventing premature failures and extending asset lifespan.

- **Improved Occupant Comfort:** Integrate BAS data with CMMS to react proactively to issues impacting occupant comfort, ensuring a consistently positive experience.

Bridging the Gap: Integration Solutions:

- **Direct Integration:** Establishing a direct data exchange between CMMS and BAS through APIs or standardized protocols.

- **Third-Party Integration Platforms:** Utilizing middleware solutions to facilitate communication and data exchange between disparate systems.

- **Cloud-Based Solutions:** Employing cloud-based CMMS and BAS offering built-in integration capabilities and centralized data access.

Navigating the Terminology:

- **Work Order:** A formal request for maintenance or repair within the facility, generated by BAS alerts or scheduled maintenance plans within the CMMS.

- **Preventive Maintenance:** Planned maintenance tasks performed regularly to prevent equipment failures, often triggered by data-driven insights from the integrated systems.

- **Corrective Maintenance:** Repairing or replacing equipment after a failure occurs, ideally minimized through effective preventive maintenance strategies.

- **Key Performance Indicators (KPIs):** Metrics used to track and measure the performance of systems and maintenance activities, often derived from integrated data.

- **Data Analytics:** Analyzing large datasets from CMMS and BAS to identify trends, optimize operations, and make data-driven decisions.

Real-World Success Stories:

- **Case Study 1: Manufacturing Facility:** A manufacturing plant integrated CMMS and BAS to implement predictive maintenance, reducing downtime by 30% and increasing production efficiency by 15%.

- **Case Study 2: Hospital Network:** A hospital network combined CMMS and BAS data to optimize energy consumption in HVAC systems, achieving a 20% reduction in energy costs and improved patient comfort.

Expert Insights:

- **Maintenance Manager:** "Integration has been a game-changer. We can now anticipate issues before they happen, saving us time, money, and ensuring smooth operations."

- **Sustainability Consultant:** "CMMS and BAS integration empowers data-driven decisions, fostering a more sustainable and efficient facility through optimized resource utilization."

Remember, a holistic approach is key. By integrating CMMS and BAS, you can unlock a wealth of benefits, empowering your facility to operate smarter, optimize resource utilization, and create a more sustainable and efficient environment for all occupants.

Bonus Section:

Action Items:

- Assess your current CMMS and BAS capabilities and identify integration potential.

- Research and evaluate different integration solutions based on your needs and budget.

- Develop a clear implementation plan outlining objectives, timelines, and responsible parties.

- Ensure data standardization and consistency across both systems for seamless integration.

- Train staff on utilizing the integrated system and leveraging its functionalities.

Additional Terms:

- **Building Management System (BMS):** A broader term encompassing BAS with additional functionalities like fire safety and security systems.

- **Internet of Things (IoT):** Network of interconnected devices generating data within the facility, further enriching the data pool for analysis.

- **Digital Twin:** A virtual replica of the physical facility created using data from CMMS and BAS, enabling simulations and optimization initiatives.

- **Artificial Intelligence (AI):** Utilizing AI algorithms to analyze data, identify patterns, and automate decision-making within the integrated system.

Chapter 14
Compliance and Risk Mitigation
Proactive Measures for a Safe and Secure Environment

In today's complex world, facility management demands constant vigilance towards maintaining compliance with regulations, proactively mitigating risks, and fostering a safe and secure environment for occupants, staff, and assets. This chapter delves into essential strategies and resources to navigate the ever-evolving landscape of compliance and risk management, empowering you to create a resilient and secure haven within your facility.

Understanding the Compliance Landscape:
- **Identify Applicable Regulations:** Research and understand regulations relevant to your

facility type, location, and operations, including building codes, fire safety standards, environmental regulations, data privacy laws, and accessibility guidelines.

- **Stay Informed:** Regularly monitor regulatory updates and changes to ensure ongoing compliance. Utilize resources like professional associations, government websites, and legal counsel for timely updates.

- **Develop Compliance Processes:** Implement documented procedures and checklists to ensure consistent adherence to regulations, assign clear responsibilities, and maintain accurate records.

Embracing Proactive Risk Management:
- **Conduct Risk Assessments:** Regularly assess potential threats and vulnerabilities within your facility, encompassing fire hazards, security breaches, natural disasters, and occupational safety concerns.

- **Develop Mitigation Strategies:** Implement proactive measures to minimize identified risks, such as fire safety protocols, cybersecurity safeguards, emergency preparedness plans, and regular equipment maintenance.

- **Invest in Staff Training:** Educate and train staff on relevant regulations, safety procedures, risk mitigation strategies, and emergency response protocols.

- **Promote a Culture of Safety:** Foster a culture of safety by encouraging open communication, incident reporting, and continuous improvement in risk management practices.

Leveraging Technology for Enhanced Security:

- **Access Control Systems:** Implement secure access control systems with keyless entry, mobile credentials, and biometric authentication for authorized personnel.

- **Surveillance Systems:** Consider video surveillance systems strategically placed to deter unauthorized access, monitor activity, and assist in incident investigations.

- **Cybersecurity Solutions:** Deploy robust cybersecurity measures to protect your network, data, and systems from cyberattacks, including firewalls, encryption, and employee training.

- **Building Automation Systems (BAS):** Utilize BAS capabilities like automated fire alarms, intrusion detection, and environmental monitoring to proactively address potential safety concerns.

Real-World Case Studies:
- **Case Study 1: Enhanced Fire Safety:** A hospital implemented advanced fire detection and suppression systems coupled with regular fire drills and evacuation training, significantly reducing fire risk and ensuring occupant safety.

- **Case Study 2: Data Breach Prevention:** A retail chain invested in robust cybersecurity measures, employee training, and data encryption procedures, preventing a potential data breach and safeguarding customer information.

Insights from Compliance and Security Experts:
- **Compliance Officer:** "Compliance isn't just about avoiding fines; it's about creating a safe and responsible environment for everyone. Proactive

measures are key."

- **Security Consultant:** "Technology serves as a valuable tool, but continuous training, clear procedures, and a culture of vigilance are crucial for effective risk mitigation."

Remember, compliance and risk management are ongoing processes. By remaining informed, proactively addressing potential threats, and fostering a culture of safety, you can create a facility that prioritizes the well-being of occupants, staff, and assets while navigating the ever-changing compliance landscape.

Bonus Section:

Action Items:

- Conduct a comprehensive compliance audit to identify any gaps or areas for improvement.

- Develop a risk management plan outlining identified risks, mitigation strategies, and responsible parties.

- Implement emergency preparedness plans and conduct regular drills to ensure staff and occupants are prepared for different scenarios.

- Partner with compliance and security professionals for expert guidance and support.

- Regularly review and update your compliance and risk management strategies to reflect changes in regulations and evolving threats.

Additional Terms:

- **Hazard:** A potential source of harm, such as fire, electrical hazards, or slips and falls.

- **Incident:** An event that has the potential to cause harm, damage, or loss.

- **Business Continuity Plan (BCP):** A plan outlining how your facility will continue operations in the event of a disruptive event.

- **Disaster Recovery Plan (DRP):** A plan outlining how to recover IT systems and data after a major disruption.

- **Safety Data Sheet (SDS):** A document providing information on the hazards of specific chemicals used in the facility.

FAQs:

- What are the most common compliance challenges faced by facility managers?

- How can I ensure accurate documentation and record-keeping for compliance purposes?

- What resources are available to help me stay informed about evolving regulations and best practices?

Bonus Bonus Section: Ensuring Accessibility and Inclusion through ADA Compliance

Creating a facility that is accessible and inclusive for everyone, regardless of ability, is not just a legal requirement but also a moral imperative. This section delves into the key aspects of the Americans with Disabilities Act (ADA) and its implications for facility management, empowering you to navigate compliance and foster a welcoming environment for all occupants.

Understanding the ADA:

- **Title III:** Covers public accommodations and commercial facilities, mandating equal access for individuals with disabilities to all goods, services, and facilities.

- **Accessibility Standards:** The ADA Accessibility Guidelines (ADAAG) outline specific requirements for accessible design features, including ramps, elevators, accessible restrooms, braille signage, and assistive technology.

- **Reasonable Accommodations:** Entities covered by the ADA must provide reasonable accommodations to ensure effective and equal participation of individuals with disabilities.

Key Terms:

- **Accessibility:** Design and construction features that enable individuals with disabilities to independently access, navigate, and utilize a facility.

- **Barrier:** Any physical, architectural, or communication obstacle that hinders access or participation for individuals with disabilities.

- **Universal Design:** Designing spaces and products usable by all people, regardless of ability, eliminating the need for adaptations.

- **Assistive Technology:** Devices and equipment that enhance the ability of individuals with disabilities to interact with their environment.

- **Certified Access Specialist (CASp):** Professionals trained in identifying and evaluating accessibility barriers within facilities.

Compliance Strategies:

- **Conduct an Accessibility Audit:** Evaluate your facility against the ADAAG standards to identify potential barriers and areas for improvement.

- **Develop a Transition Plan:** Create a plan outlining steps to address identified barriers, prioritizing critical areas and allocating resources effectively.

- **Partner with Accessibility Professionals:** Collaborate with architects, engineers, and CASps for expert guidance on design, construction, and compliance matters.

- **Provide Staff Training:** Educate staff on disability etiquette, communication best practices, and how to assist individuals with disabilities effectively.

- **Continuously Monitor and Improve:** Regularly evaluate accessibility features, update policies and procedures, and remain informed about evolving standards.

Beyond Compliance: Building an Inclusive Culture:

- **Accessibility goes beyond physical barriers.** Embrace diverse perspectives and actively involve individuals with disabilities in planning and decision-making processes.

- **Promote disability awareness and sensitivity.** Organize educational workshops, create awareness campaigns, and celebrate diversity within your facility.

- **Focus on inclusive design solutions.** Implement universal design principles whenever possible, creating a welcoming and usable environment for everyone.

- **Partner with disability advocacy organizations.** Collaborate with local organizations to gain insights and build meaningful partnerships.

Remember, accessibility is not just about meeting legal requirements; it's about creating a welcoming and inclusive environment for all. By proactively addressing accessibility concerns, fostering a culture of awareness and acceptance, and continuously seeking improvement, you can contribute to a more equitable and just society.

Additional Resources:
- The National Center for Universal Design:

- The ADA National Network: https://adata.org/

- The American Association of People with Disabilities (AAPD): https://www.aapd.com/

Bonus Bonus Bonus Section: The Importance and Role of EHS in Facility Management

Environment, Health, and Safety (EHS) plays a crucial role in facility management, encompassing a holistic approach to creating a safe, healthy, and environmentally responsible work environment for occupants, staff, and the surrounding community.

Understanding the Significance of EHS:
- **Protects People and Assets:** Implementing robust EHS practices minimizes workplace injuries, illnesses, and environmental incidents, safeguarding human well-being and facil-

ity assets.

- **Reduces Costs:** Proactive EHS management prevents accidents, minimizes regulatory fines, and lowers insurance premiums, contributing to cost savings and financial sustainability.

- **Enhances Compliance:** Staying informed and adherent to environmental regulations, health and safety standards, and waste management guidelines ensures legal compliance and avoids potential penalties.

- **Boosts Reputation and Sustainability:** Demonstrating commitment to EHS principles fosters a positive reputation, attracts responsible tenants and occupants, and aligns with broader sustainability goals.

Key EHS Roles and Responsibilities:

- **EHS Manager:** Oversees the development and implementation of EHS policies, programs, and procedures, ensuring compliance with regulations and best practices.

- **Safety Officer:** Identifies and assesses workplace

hazards, conducts safety inspections, investigates incidents, and provides safety training to staff.

- **Environmental Coordinator:** Manages waste disposal, energy efficiency initiatives, and environmental compliance programs, minimizing environmental impact.

- **Industrial Hygienist:** Evaluates potential health risks associated with hazardous materials and processes, recommending safeguards and monitoring air quality.

- **Emergency Response Team:** Prepares and trains for emergency situations, such as fires, chemical spills, or natural disasters.

Common EHS Terms:
- **Hazard:** A potential source of harm, such as electrical hazards, exposure to chemicals, or slips and falls.

- **Risk:** The likelihood of a hazard causing harm, considering its severity and the probability of occurrence.

- **Personal Protective Equipment**

(PPE): Equipment worn to minimize exposure to workplace hazards, like gloves, masks, or safety glasses.

- **Safety Data Sheet (SDS):** A document providing information on the hazards of specific chemicals used in the facility.

- **Material Safety Data Sheet (MSDS):** An older term used for SDS.

- **Incident:** An event that has the potential to cause harm, damage, or loss.

- **Near Miss:** An event that could have resulted in an incident but luckily did not.

- **Environmental Impact Assessment (EIA):** A study evaluating the potential environmental impact of a project or activity.

- **Sustainability:** Meeting the needs of the present without compromising the ability of future generations to meet their own needs.

Enhancing Your EHS Program:
- **Conduct Regular Risk Assessments:** Proac-

tively identify potential hazards and implement preventive measures to minimize risks.

- **Invest in Training and Education:** Train staff on EHS policies, procedures, and safe work practices to foster a culture of safety and awareness.

- **Promote Employee Engagement:** Encourage open communication, incident reporting, and continuous improvement efforts in EHS practices.

- **Utilize Technology:** Leverage technology for data collection, incident reporting, and safety training to enhance program effectiveness.

- **Seek Expert Guidance:** Partner with EHS professionals and consultants for specialized advice and support.

Remember, EHS is not a standalone program; it's an integral part of responsible facility management. By prioritizing EHS, you can create a safer, healthier, and more sustainable environment for everyone, while contributing to positive social and environmental impact.

Additional Resources:
- The Occupational Safety and Health Adminis-

tration (OSHA): https://www.osha.gov/

- The National Institute for Occupational Safety and Health (NIOSH): https://www.cdc.gov/niosh/

- The United States Environmental Protection Agency (EPA): https://www.epa.gov

Chapter 15
Continuous Learning
Sharpening Your Skills and Embracing Adaptability in a Dynamic Landscape

The facility management landscape is constantly evolving, driven by technological advancements, shifting regulations, and emerging best practices. In this dynamic environment, continuous learning and adaptability are essential for success. This chapter delves into the importance of ongoing professional development, explores various learning avenues, and equips you with the skills to navigate change and thrive in an ever-changing world.

Why Continuous Learning Matters:

- **Stay Ahead of the Curve:** Master new technologies, adapt to evolving regulations, and implement best practices to ensure your facility operations remain efficient, compliant, and competitive.

- **Enhance Your Skillset:** Expand your knowledge base, refine existing skills, and acquire new competencies to excel in your role and explore career advancement opportunities.

- **Promote Innovation:** Foster a culture of learning within your team, encouraging exploration of new ideas and solutions to optimize facility operations and occupant experience.

- **Increase Personal Satisfaction:** Embrace the challenge of continuous learning, gain a sense of accomplishment, and experience the joy of expanding your professional horizons.

Exploring Learning Avenues:
- **Formal Education:** Enroll in certificate programs, professional development courses, or pursue higher education degrees relevant to your field.

- **Industry Associations:** Join professional organizations like IFMA, BOMA, or NAA, participate in conferences, workshops, and webinars offered by these associations.

- **Online Learning Platforms:** Utilize online platforms like LinkedIn Learning, Udemy, or Coursera to access a vast library of on-demand courses and tutorials.

- **Mentorship and Coaching:** Seek guidance from experienced professionals in your field through mentorship programs or coaching sessions.

- **Networking Events:** Attend industry events, conferences, and networking gatherings to connect with peers, exchange knowledge, and stay informed about emerging trends.

- **Industry Publications:** Subscribe to industry magazines, newsletters, and blogs to stay updated on the latest news, research, and best practices.

Developing Key Skills for Adaptability:

- **Critical Thinking:** Analyze information objectively, identify problems, and develop effective solutions in response to changing circumstances.

- **Problem-Solving:** Approach challenges creatively, think outside the box, and devise innovative solutions to overcome obstacles.

- **Communication:** Clearly articulate your ideas, actively listen to others, and effectively communicate with diverse stakeholders.

- **Collaboration:** Work effectively with colleagues, partners, and external service providers to achieve shared goals.

- **Digital Literacy:** Embrace technology, adapt to new software and tools, and leverage them to enhance your work efficiency and decision-making.

- **Time Management:** Prioritize tasks effectively, manage your schedule efficiently, and adapt to unexpected changes while maintaining productivity.

Navigating Change with Confidence:
- **Embrace a Growth Mindset:** View challenges as opportunities to learn and grow, fostering a positive and open attitude towards change.

- **Be Proactive:** Stay informed about industry trends, anticipate potential changes, and proactively prepare yourself and your team for upcoming shifts.

- **Communicate Effectively:** Keep stakeholders informed about changes, address concerns transparently, and actively solicit feedback to ensure a smooth transition.

- **Seek Support:** Utilize available resources, leverage your network, and don't hesitate to seek help from colleagues or mentors when facing challenges.

- **Celebrate Successes:** Recognize and celebrate individual and team achievements in adapting to change, reinforcing a positive and adaptable culture.

Remember, continuous learning is not a one-time event; it's a lifelong journey. By embracing opportunities to learn, develop new skills, and adapt to change, you can ensure your success in an ever-evolving facility management landscape.

Bonus Section:

Action Items:

- Identify your skill gaps and areas for improvement based on your career goals and current role.

- Develop a personalized learning plan outlining specific courses, resources, or events you will engage in.

- Allocate dedicated time for learning activities within your weekly schedule.

- Actively participate in industry events, conferences, and networking opportunities.

- Reflect on your learning journey and adjust your plan as needed to ensure continuous growth and development.

Additional Resources:

- Building Owners and Managers Association (BOMA): https://www.boma.org/

- National Apartment Association (NAA): https://naant.org/dashboard/

- LinkedIn Learning: https://www.linkedin.com/learning/

- Udemy: https://www.udemy.com/

- Coursera: [https://www.coursera.org/](https://www.coursera.org

Bonus Bonus Section

Facility Management: Swiss Army Knife or Specialized Sharpshooter?

The Allure of the Swiss Army Knife:

In the dynamic world of facility management, being a "Swiss Army Knife" professional holds undeniable appeal. With a diverse skillset and the ability to tackle various tasks, you offer undeniable value. You can troubleshoot electrical issues, fix leaky faucets, manage budgets, analyze data, and handle tenant concerns – all within your stride. This versatility shines in:

- **Small teams:** When resources are limited, your adaptability becomes crucial.

- **Fast-paced environments:** You can quickly switch gears and solve unexpected problems without relying on specialists.

- **Emergencies:** Your diverse skillset allows you to

react quickly and effectively to unforeseen situations.

The Power of Specialization:

However, Bruce Lee's wisdom rings true in facility management too. Imagine a technician who has practiced maintaining HVAC systems for years, honing their expertise to identify subtle inefficiencies and optimize performance. Their deep understanding translates to:

- **Superior efficiency:** Specialized knowledge allows for faster, more accurate diagnoses and problem-solving.

- **Advanced solutions:** Deep expertise opens doors to implementing complex, cutting-edge solutions.

- **Greater impact:** Specialization allows you to become a leader within your field, influencing industry practices and standards.

Finding the Balance:

Neither pure specialization nor unbridled generalization provides the perfect answer. The optimal approach lies in a nuanced understanding of your role and environment:

- **Identify core competencies:** Determine the essential skills required for your specific role and facility type.

- **Deepen expertise:** Within your core competencies, identify areas for specialization that offer significant impact.

- **Maintain adaptability:** Cultivate a "learning agility" mindset, allowing you to acquire new skills as needed for unexpected challenges.

- **Build a complementary team:** Surround yourself with individuals who possess complementary skills, fostering a well-rounded team dynamic.

Remember, true mastery lies not just in possessing many tools, but in knowing when and how to use them effectively. Embrace your ability to learn and adapt, while simultaneously seeking opportunities to refine your knowledge and expertise in areas that offer the most significant value for your role and facility. Ultimately, your personal and professional growth trajectory should be guided by a strategic blend of the Swiss Army Knife's versatility and the sharpshooter's focused excellence.

Additional Considerations:

- **Team dynamics:** Assess your team's skillsets and identify any gaps that specialization can address.

- **Career aspirations:** Consider your long-term career goals and how specialization can propel you towards them.

- **Lifelong learning:** Regardless of your chosen path, commit to continuous learning to stay relevant and adaptable in the evolving facility management landscape.

By thoughtfully navigating the pros and cons of specialization and generalization, you can unlock your full potential as a facility management professional, contributing significantly to the efficient, sustainable, and thriving future of your facility.

Chapter 16
Mentorship
Passing the Torch and Giving Back to the Profession

In the ever-evolving world of facility management, knowledge and experience are invaluable assets. Yet, no leader reigns forever. This chapter delves into the profound impact of mentorship, exploring how passing the torch ensures the continued success of both individuals and the profession.

The Power of Mentorship:

Mentorship fosters a dynamic exchange, enriching both mentor and mentee. As a **mentor**, you share your insights, guidance, and experience, shaping the next generation of facility professionals. As a **mentee**, you gain invaluable wisdom, accelerate your learning curve, and build meaningful connections within the industry. This two-way exchange ultimately benefits:

- **Individuals:** Mentees gain skills, confidence, and career guidance, while mentors experience personal growth through teaching and sharing.

- **Facilities:** By nurturing talent, mentorship ensures a pipeline of skilled professionals equipped to tackle future challenges.

- **The Profession:** By fostering knowledge transfer and professional development, mentorship elevates the standards and expertise within the facility management field.

Identifying Your Future Successor:

A true leader recognizes that being **irreplaceable hinders your own growth and the team's potential**. The ability to identify and cultivate your successor is a hallmark of effective leadership. Look for these qualities in potential mentees:

- **Proactive Learning:** A genuine desire to learn, ask questions, and actively seek opportunities for growth.

- **Strong Work Ethic:** Dedication, commitment to excellence, and a willingness to go the extra mile.

- **Leadership Potential:** Demonstrates initiative, problem-solving skills, and the ability to inspire and motivate others.

- **Alignment with Values:** Shares your professional values and vision for the future of the facility or organization.

Mentoring for Succession:

Effective mentorship for succession goes beyond occasional advice. Invest in your mentee's growth through:

- **Delegation:** Gradually entrust them with increasing responsibilities, providing constructive feedback and support.

- **Knowledge Sharing:** Share your expertise through structured training, project collaboration, and open communication.

- **Networking Opportunities:** Introduce them to key industry figures and facilitate their participation in professional development events.

- **Leadership Exposure:** Assign leadership roles in projects or committees, fostering their confidence and decision-making skills.

Remember, succession planning is not a one-time event; it's an ongoing process. Regularly assess your mentee's progress, adjust your approach as needed, and celebrate their achievements as they become ready to assume your mantle.

Beyond Mentorship: Other Pillars of Giving Back:

Mentorship is just one way to contribute to the profession. Consider these additional avenues:

- **Speaking Engagements:** Share your expertise at industry conferences or workshops, inspiring and educating the next generation.

- **Volunteer Work:** Offer your skills and experience to non-profit organizations or industry initiatives.

- **Writing and Content Creation:** Contribute articles, blog posts, or white papers sharing your knowledge and insights.

- **Serving on Industry Boards:** Lend your voice and expertise to shape the future of the profession through industry associations.

Closing Thoughts:

Facility management is not just a job; it's a dynamic and rewarding career path. By embracing mentorship and actively contributing to the growth of others, you leave a lasting legacy, ensuring the continued success of both the profession and the individuals who shape it. Remember, **mentorship is not about creating clones; it's about empowering the next generation to rise above and beyond.** With this spirit of collaboration and knowledge sharing, you can ensure the facility management field thrives for generations to come.

Additional Resources:

- Building Owners and Managers Association (BOMA) Young Professionals Group

- Facility Management Journal

Essential Resources:

- **Industry Associations:** Engage with professional organizations like BOMA, and NAA for industry news, certifications, events, and networking opportunities.

- **Publications and Websites:** Subscribe to industry magazines like Facility Management Journal, Buildings, and Property Management Magazine for insights, best practices, and case studies.

- **Online Learning Platforms:** Utilize platforms like LinkedIn Learning, Udemy, and Coursera to access a vast library of courses, tutorials, and webinars on various facility management topics.

- **Podcasts and Blogs:** Stay informed and inspired by industry-specific podcasts and blogs, offering diverse perspectives and actionable tips.

- **Research and Reports:** Access valuable research reports and white papers from organizations like USGBC, ASHRAE, and FM Global for data-driven insights and industry trends.

Technology Tools to Empower You:

- **Computerized Maintenance Management Systems (CMMS):** Streamline work orders, manage preventive maintenance, and track facility assets.

- **Building Automation Systems (BAS):** Optimize energy efficiency, monitor equipment performance, and automate facility functions.

- **Data Analytics Tools:** Analyze facility data to identify trends, optimize operations, and make data-driven decisions.

- **Mobile Apps:** Utilize mobile apps for inspections, reporting, tenant communication, and on-the-go facility management tasks.

- **Virtual Reality (VR) and Augmented Reality (AR):** Explore innovative technologies for remote inspections, facility design visualization, and training purposes.

Maintaining Motivation and Inspiration:

- **Connect with Industry Leaders:** Follow renowned facility management professionals on social media, attend their webinars, or read their books for valuable insights and inspiration.

- **Participate in Industry Awards:** Submit your projects or initiatives for industry awards to gain recognition and showcase your achievements.

- **Attend Industry Events:** Network with peers, learn about cutting-edge solutions, and participate in workshops and conferences to stay motivated and energized.

- **Seek Mentorship or Coaching:** Find a mentor or coach to guide your career development, provide feedback, and offer support.

- **Volunteer or Give Back:** Share your expertise and contribute to the profession by volunteering your time or skills to industry initiatives or non-profit organizations.

Remember, facility management is not just a job; it's a dynamic and impactful career. By continuously learning, embracing new technologies, and staying connected with the industry, you can make a significant contribution to creating efficient, sustainable, and thriving facilities for all.

Never stop learning, growing, and inspiring others. The future of facility management is bright, and you have the potential to shape it for the better.

Chapter 17
Embarking on Your Facility Management Odyssey
Next Steps and Beyond

Congratulations! You've reached the end of this exploration into the fascinating world of facility management. By now, you have a foundational understanding of the core principles, diverse landscapes, and ever-evolving nature of this dynamic field. But the journey doesn't end here. It's just the beginning of your own unique Facility Management Odyssey.

So, what are the next steps?
Take action:

- **Refine your focus:** Reflect on the specific areas that resonate with you – healthcare facilities, commercial properties, or perhaps the intricacies of boutique hotels. This self-awareness will guide your career path.

- **Build your knowledge base:** Delve deeper into the industry resources mentioned throughout this handbook. Attend conferences, join professional associations, and explore online communities to stay updated and network with fellow FM enthusiasts.

- **Hone your skills:** Consider pursuing relevant certifications like CFM or specialized credentials aligned with your area of interest. Invest in online courses, workshops, or volunteer opportunities to gain practical experience.

- **Showcase your value:** Craft a compelling resume and LinkedIn profile that highlights your skills and relevant experiences. Don't underestimate the power of a strong online presence in today's job market.

- **Start your journey:** Explore entry-level positions or internships to gain hands-on experience and build your professional network. Remember, every journey begins with a single step.

What can you expect?

Facility management is a career unlike any other. It offers:

- **Variety and challenge:** No two days are the same. Be prepared to tackle unexpected problems, implement innovative solutions, and thrive in a dynamic environment.

- **Continuous learning:** The field is constantly evolving with new technologies, regulations, and best practices. Be ready to embrace lifelong learning and adapt to change.

- **Making a difference:** Your work directly impacts the comfort, safety, and productivity of those who use the facilities you manage. Knowing you contribute to their well-being can be incredibly rewarding.

- **Diverse career paths:** The possibilities are endless! Specialize in a specific industry, move into leadership roles, or even become an entrepreneur

– the choice is yours.

Remember:

- **Passion is key:** This field demands dedication and a genuine interest in creating and maintaining functional, sustainable, and inspiring spaces.

- **Stay resilient:** Challenges are inevitable, but your ability to learn, adapt, and persevere will define your success.

- **Never stop exploring:** The journey of a Facility Manager is ongoing. Embrace new knowledge, network with peers, and contribute to the continuous evolution of the profession.

High-Level Advice for FM Excellence:

- **Become a strategic thinker:** Don't just manage facilities; **shape their future**. Think like a business partner, aligning facility strategy with organizational goals and maximizing value.

- **Embrace innovation:** Be an early adopter of new technologies like AI, IoT, and automation. Identify solutions that optimize efficiency, sustainability, and occupant experience.

- **Develop your financial acumen:** Understand budgeting, cost control, and return on investment (ROI) calculations. Demonstrate the financial impact of your decisions.

- **Cultivate leadership skills:** Lead by example, motivate your team, and foster a collaborative environment. Effective communication and conflict resolution are crucial.

- **Network strategically:** Build relationships with industry leaders, mentors, and potential clients. Participate in professional organizations and attend industry events.

- **Become a lifelong learner:** Stay updated on emerging trends, regulations, and best practices. Pursue relevant certifications and actively seek new knowledge.

- **Specialize for impact:** Hone your expertise in a specific area like healthcare, sustainable facilities, or high-tech environments. Become a sought-after specialist.

- **Think globally:** The FM landscape is expanding internationally. Develop cultural sensitivity and explore opportunities beyond your borders.

Lucrative Opportunities in FM:

- **Executive-level positions:** Chief Facility Officer, Regional Facilities Director, Global Head of Facilities - these roles demand strategic leadership, complex problem-solving, and proven track records, and come with hefty compensation packages.

- **Consulting:** Establish your own consultancy, offering specialized expertise to diverse clients. Build a strong reputation and attract high-value projects.

- **Facility Management as a Service (FMaaS):** Develop innovative service models and leverage technology to cater to specific industry needs. Disrupt the traditional FM landscape and reap the rewards.

- **Entrepreneurship:** Identify unmet needs in the FM industry and develop innovative solutions. Starting your own company can be a lucrative path for the truly enterprising.

Remember:

Reaching the six-figure realm requires dedication, exceptional skills, and strategic career planning. But with the right mindset, the willingness to go above and beyond, and the advice laid out here, you can unlock the full potential of your FM journey.

So, are you ready to embark on this exciting path? Seize the opportunities, embrace the challenges, and create your own success story in the dynamic world of Facility Management. The future is yours to shape!

Disclaimer:

Reaching six-figure earnings is not guaranteed and depends on individual skills, experience, and career path. However, pursuing FM at the highest levels offers significant potential for financial success.

Thank You:

I extend a heartfelt thank you for embarking on this journey with us. We welcome you with open arms and encourage you to explore, innovate, and shape the future of this dynamic field. Remember, the key to a successful Facility Management Odyssey lies in your passion, dedication, and continuous pursuit of excellence.